A GAL CAN DREAM CAN'T SHE?

Letters of Hélène Stauffer Hero
To Her Daughters 1956-1962

Edited by Hélène Hero Rufty,
John LeBourgeois, Mimi Hero LeBourgeois
Ashton LeBourgeois

Copyright 2016 Mimi LeBourgeois
All rights reserved

Alvin and Hélène

Hélène Stauffer Hero (1913-1965) began writing these letters when her eldest daughter left New Orleans for college in 1956. She and her husband Alvin had five daughters. Hélène, when she went to Randolph-Macon College in Lynchburg, Virginia, was almost eighteen. Mimi was sixteen, Celeste fourteen, Ann not quite nine, and Caroline (called Crin) had just turned four. The letters told the younger Hélène all the news of home, in the Garden District of New Orleans. A year later when Mimi went off to Smith College in Northampton, Massachusetts, Hélène made a carbon copy. Three years later Celeste followed Mimi to Smith and was added to the list. The fifty-eight letters plus one postcard run from the fall of 1956 to the early spring of 1962, before Ann and Crin were old enough to go to college.

The letters are mostly long, rich in detail, and full of triumphs and misadventures. They catalogue a lot of parties and late night activities, particularly after Hélène became chair of the Women's Board of the New Orleans Symphony Orchestra in 1957. A list at the end of the book identifies some of the people mentioned.

Hélène thought of herself as a writer and sent her stories and poems to The New Yorker. As she said, "A gal can dream, can't she?" We think her best work is in her letters, now in print.

Mimi 19, Hélène 20, Celeste 17, Crin 7, and Ann 11. Ca 1959

Letter 1

Postmark 10 Sept 56
Sun nite

Well, it's very nice knowing your friends -- i.e. Molly & Barney & Walter, came here Sun. afternoon to see how we were bearing up under your departure. Of course, after 2 or 3 drinks I forgot it when I had children here, and Walter said why wasn't I crying & I said I had such good control. And then M.L. & Warren came over to try & fill the void & we ended up by going over to their house for spaghetti &

wine & I thought I'd see how your P.O. number looked on an envelope so here I am in bed writing to you so you will have a letter anyway two days or at least one day after you arrive. But anyway, the firstest is the worstest, whether it is a-borning or a-leaving so friend you have given me the double whammy & I still love you, so you must be pretty good.

Sunnyside Farm, Gap, PA "The Gap"

Mimi had lunch with a friend from camp & Ann went over to Sydney's & hasn't come back yet & Crin is popping balloons on the floor & the Kirby's are making a lot of noise across the street which we can hear because it's so cool & we do not have the air-conditioning on, & the bugs are flying all around, which I hate.

I told Walter Ike offered you the Gap on Thanksgiving for a house party & he let out a whoop & a holler you could hear for a mile & his eyes got an awful gleam, & I knew I had made a dreadful mistake. And Barney kept talking about the Waldorf & Walter kept talking about the Biltmore & he wanted to know if you made your reservations yet and I said as if I knew.

I made a deal over at the Posey's tonight. We are going to get their 6 burner 2 oven stove which they are pitching when the new kitchen gets going. Your father thinks it's a good one, & I am so sly I have been keeping it under my lid for some time & no one knows. If we get rid of our electric one pops won't be so worried when the gals go off at night & leave a light burning which puts us in the high-electrical bracket, so all-in-all it will eliminate a tiny part of the friction in the running of the house.

I hope you get used to this uneducated scrawl. After all, remember I am a McGhee girl and can do no better.

Love, kisses
Ma & Pa & Mimi & Celeste & Ann & Crin

Ah! Elvis is ON !!

Letter 2

Postmark 14 Sept 56
Thursday

Dear Hel

We all enjoyed your letter that came today. What has been going on via rushing? I am enclosing the LSU finals, in case you did not hear of everyone. Kat. Geiger does not seem to be listed. Alvin suggested because she is in Gretna not N.O. but feel sure if she were in she would be with N.O.

I went over to Vicki's to bring her her present. She wasn't in, but sat & had a gin & tonic with Va. and had one of those round-robins with her. Seems she said V said Mimi said Mrs. Schultz said the woman at Wellesley took a dislike to V & that was why she was turned down. And Virginia said Wellesley was the one place they did not have an interview, so there I was caught and horrified that Mimi would repeat such. So came home to Mimi & found Mrs. S. did not tell that to her but to another girl, if it is true at all. Gads! I wish Va. would keep these girlish confidences to herself. Gave Mimi Hell for repeating disagreeable things.

Walter called to say goodbye. Hope he likes it at Al & Barbara's. Suzie Isacks left tonight. She was a grand visitor and refused to let us do a thing for her. Feel awful now that she insisted on studying on Celeste's bed, and I found her on the floor of Mimi's room last night. Wouldn't use Mimi's desk. I finally gave up insisting & said she had good sense & knew what she wanted to do. Pearce Hurley drove her home from school every day. Must like girls called Susie. She had a fainting spell this morning and I felt flopping -- helpless. Made her go upstairs & lie down and take an aspirin. She slept a bit and then said she wanted to go to school & was most apologetic because of all the trouble. Wrote her a note & of course spelled her name Isaacs! After all these years I feel quite remiss at knowing how it was spelled. By the way, it's corner. Your set up sounds very nice. What have you decided about room decoration?

Going to Cyn's for dinner Sat. night with some of the 21 French parliamentarians who are in town. She asked weeks ago, and M.L. asked us a few days ago to come to her house as she has 2 to entertain. Bad luck!

Let me know about rushing

                              Love,
                                    Ma

Letter 3

Postmark 19 Sep 56
Tuesday

Dear Helene

We have all settled down again after a glorious Sat with the Frenchmen. We left Cynthia's party, as her two men left early & went over on to M.L. & Warren's where things were very gay. She had two Frenchmen & two State Dept. men, and we ended up with eggs, wine & coffee in our yard at 5 A. M. I think they all had a marvelous time & it will take them two days to forget N.O. as they catch up on their sleep.

Side Garden at 1213 Third Street

Vicki came by to tell us goodbye and she is very excited. Life has been a little dull with only Althea to play around with. The rumor is that Emmy didn't make anything.

The people at Colo. must be saps! Molly called that Walter is having a good time at Alfred & Barbara's. Barney called him Sat & a cocktail party was going full swing & it was just like home! I think he has found a room in the dorm. Molly sounds very pleased about it. They telephoned that Mimi is getting Tri G, so I'll go there at 2:30 tomorrow for Assembly.

M.L. & I took Lou to the hospital today. She is scared to death, but puts up a very big front and is very gay. Her operation is at 8 tomorrow. She didn't want to go to bed when she first got there, thought she would be able to sit up in a chair. Kept telling the nurses it was first time in 30 yrs. etc. Taunteen - Anita - Myrthé arrived, so we left.

Telephone us collect next Sunday & let us know how you are, etc. Be nice to hear your voice. Ann started school, but

Hélène Stauffer Hero

there seems to be no hope for Crin this year. Someone presented her with a kitten & she came in the house cradling the kitty with her skirt & was so excited I let her keep it. Ann has a turtle, so we seem to be full of pets at the moment. Full for us, that is.
.

It's the <u>telephone</u> not getting answered that drives me <u>mad</u>.

Love,
Hélène

I didn't see my picture finished. Just had Holmes send it to you. I hope it's not too repulsive.

Letter 4

Postmark 26 Sep 56
Monday

Dear Hélène

We weathered "Flossie" without more damage than a torn off shutter & a broken window pane. No large limbs blew off trees, but the yard and sidewalk are of course a mess. I had to relent & let the kitten in who promptly crawled under the hot water heater. It is the scrawniest, ugliest bit of cat I have ever seen & Crin adores it -- says it bites her with its claws & if it survives her love it will be a miracle. We had the usual little people over today as there was no school, & for diversion to see M.C. I have not seen her in two days but know she has loads of company with all the girls. She is of course as cheerful as a cricket.

Jill's mother called to see if by any chance Jill had left over here a green sun dress that she wants shipped promptly before a party & her mother is calling down the line as she cannot find it. I couldn't help her a bit. Walter writes glowing letters about staying with Alfred & Barbara -- many intellectual & interesting people seem to be around all the time. Still no room at the dorms. Molly is getting embarrassed. His address is 98 Raymond Street, Cambridge, Mass c/o A.O. Hero, Jr.

Love, Ma

Letter 5

Postmark 3 Oct 56

Dear Helene

Lou came home Saturday with her trained nurse, and yesterday father had a belated birthday party for her, which I <u>forgot</u>. Molly & Barney were over for the usual Sun. drink & I was completely in a fog when the telephone rang at 2:30 & Ike said everyone was waiting. I didn't even have a present for her & Crin had to be got dressed & we had to

13

stop & buy a plant. I felt awful, Ike & Granny & ML were leaving just as we drove up. The gals had ice cream & cake downstairs & I staid up & talked. I wish I had told you before to be sure & write her. How can you do the right things if I haven't been teaching you?

I got asked to be Social Chairman for Senior Class at Newman, but I turned it down. Could see myself getting stuck with parties here. Took Telephone Chairman instead. Registered Crin & Ann both. Did I write you Mimi got Girls Govt?

The storm blew down a magnolia tree in the Dinwiddie's yard, & Martha Miles called me up & went with me and I got branches & branches to decorate the house for little Cyn's party. Sprayed them with clear plastic spray to preserve them & hope they last for 3 weeks.

Celeste is on the hunt for amoebas in the garden pond. Crin's cat seems to be the same size it was two weeks ago and it is driving me insane. Crin is so much happier with something to talk to all day. I am gritting my teeth. It's sadly ugly.

Went to the Legendre's Fri night & saw their European pictures. I fall in love with their house every time I go there, with the big porch with the glass-doors that open out into her garden. It's a wonderful combination of new-old -- our house across the river could be like it.

Sat night Tony Sciacca, one of Ike's salesmen, had us to Italian dinner -- each dish was to me a main course --

chicken -- stuffed macaroni stuffed artichokes etc ended in stuffed us. Simply gorgeous.

Love, Ma

P.S. Is it true Emmy didn't go anything?

Letter 6

Postmark 7 Oct 56
Friday

Dear Hel

Mimi has <u>the</u> pen. I have been tearing around all week at a great pace, what with Lou, mother & Marie Celeste. Luckily, Celeste is here so that relieves me except I like to go see Celeste. Poor mother all alone in bed has made me neglect Lou who has a constant train of visitors, plus the inevitable 3 <u>gals</u>. Her heart is not acting properly, so Doctor Nadler won't let her go downstairs. It is a bitter blow for her. This operation has been a lot worse than she expected. Your letter simply thrilled her -- so please write again.

Don't faint –<u>I</u> was at <u>Mrs. Manget's</u> painting on decorations for 9 O'Clocks! Mrs. Owens had been so nice about attending to Celeste's overdue invitation that I simply couldn't refuse. Came home with the usual diarreah (sp?) that a group of women give me.

Martha Miles & I have mailed the invitations to little Cyn's party -- she did some -- I sat down to do my half -- wrote Mr. and Mrs. etc etc, on all the faces turned them over, wrote In Honor of etc etc, addressed all the envelopes, finishing in 3 hours, pick up invitation, fold to put in envelope, find I had written them all upside down, went to bed in a state of collapse.

Catherine Fox had me out swimming at Metairie today. Not a soul but us -- beautiful cold water warm sun. Lunch afterwards at her house. Asked my advice about decorating her room. Usual mental block & confusion. Told her the usual blah -- blah about <u>my</u> troubles. Said she was going to write Barry to look you up -- he's at W&L -- have you seen anything of him.

I had everything all planned to take Cyn's coat to reweaver this morning but dropped it all for sin & perdition. I ordered your pictures, they are ready, and neither Mimi nor I can find the Quin letter as to where to mail them. I had to send a check to the T.P. for your subscription, which I did two weeks ago. You'll be getting it. I had them start it 1st of Oct to make things even.

Barney with Crin, Ann and Beth

Your father has Donaldsonville fair fever, so off we start in a jolly group tomorrow. Barney, Crin, Ann & Beth. I shall try to keep my temper.

Valerie Williams' mother has announced her marriage (Whittaker Riggs) as of last June, so all the cats are mewing. I have loudly announced that if any of you runs away & gets married I shall send out announcements thusly –

> Mr & Mrs Alvin Hero announce
> the marriage of their pregnant daughter

Love & kisses,
Ma

Hélène and Ike Stauffer, Hélène's Mother and Father

Letter 7

Postmark 12 Oct 56
Thursday

Dear Hel

Have taken care of all the errands except the coat. Reweavers are at strange remote places, like the 2nd block from Canal St. and I simply haven't been doing anything the last month but hospital hopping. Tomorrow will investigate the place near Carrollton Ave when I get my hair washed.

Lou's cardiograph was O.K. and the doctor said he thought the pains around the heart were gas. She is sitting up in bed, & this report should lift her morale.

About the pictures -- telephoned D & S to mail them for me & they said usually newspaper pictures were 6x8 or 8x10 or anyway something large. However, she mailed them in, and we shall see. If not, is it worth it to order 3?

Had lunch with Molly and Va. Kelly yesterday while they discussed Walt & Vick's party. The most disturbing thing to Va. seems to be V.'s waiting table.

We are still hot hot hot. I am so jealous of you off in that beautiful country.

Love, Ma

Letter 8

Postmark 23 Oct 56
Monday

Dear Hélène

I feel as if I have been neglecting you which I have, but the past two weeks have been taken up with the party, which was gorgeous! After sweating and struggling for two weeks to get the deb's lined up with dates, it all came off beautifully. My head is really swimming with compliments. The house truly looked beautiful! Martha had the florist come get the two compots & I suggested an English type bouquet with a background of green leaves & yellow flowers, and the florist made two magnificent arrangements that filled the walls with color.

Drawing Room

Granny donated two lamps & I bought some new shades, and what with 32 candles lit, and hurricane lamps lining the walk outside and Martha's mother's beautiful silver candelabra on the dining room table & a smoked turkey and a ham, the people simply raved & raved. Carmen kept dashing up to tell me that it was the first party that she has ever seen the debs relax & have a good time. We put on pop's good old jazz and there was jitterbugging later on. The 6 - 8 cocktail party broke up at 12! A very attractive Swedish couple, friends of Martha's, stayed until the bitter end, and when they said goodbye said how, when they came, they intended having a drink and leaving right away but their minds had changed rapidly! I think you could hear the noise for three blocks! My new dress was a success fou. It's emerald green chiffon backed with a wide band of emerald satin at the bottom, and a panel of chiffon attached with bows at the back. Oh well -- I feel so glowing today you must excuse all the bragging. But after all the hard work & trouble it is most gratifying. The place is a wreck today -- candle-wax over every table & white marks

Dining Room

all over the floor from spilled drinks and everything smelling cigarette-itty. It always amazes me how simple it is to put on a very little something extra -- like candles & a smoked turkey & how it lifts a party above the average with no trouble.

To get down to earth -- Lou will have to be at Touro for quite some time. She is very weak and the doctor does not want her to go home until she can take up her everyday life. She is being very brave about it, but I know it is a terrific ordeal for her. Please write her at the Touro.

 Love, Ma

Letter 9

Postmark 29 Oct 56
Monday

Dear Hel

Put this in your "small worlds" department. You remember I wrote you about the Frenchmen several weeks ago? Well, I find that one of them, a man by the name of Léon de Narbonne, has a nephew Auguste de Narbonne, who is going to W.&L. He knows Sonny Howcott. Have you met him? His uncle was one of the best looking & most attractive men I have ever seen and everyone fell for him. He came here, as I told, when we had eggs and wine

& coffee until 5 A.M. If his nephew is half as attractive he would be gorgeous.

About your ticket. You have your stub, so your father thinks you could pick up a return at your end. He does not want you to fly at that time of the year, so it will be train back.

Did you get your coat? I think they did a good job for 4.50 in fixing the patch, don't you?

Lou looks much better. She is allowed to do some walking around and her attitude is decidedly more cheerful. Your letters simply thrill her. You write such a good one.

Sèvres Urn

Guess what happened. Your father was fixing some window panes in the drawing room yesterday, and finishing up he had the ladder just leaning against the window, it slipped, he fell flat, but did fortunately not hurt himself, and the ladder crashed the Sèvres urn! Gads!! I took it to Mr. Diamond today & it is going to take a cool $140 to fix it back.

M.L's kitchen is at last being fixed. She is now cooking on a hot plate in the living room, & washing dishes in the lavatory. We bought her beautiful stove from her, so now I can cook two different kinds of eggs in the morning -- more if necessary. I think we are going to have a tremendous pay-back party with Molly & Barney, complete with band, some time in Dec. It was your father's idea & it sounds fun, if I don't jitter to pieces between now and it.

Ike sent you a sweater from Lancaster but it is too small -- so I am sending them back & suggested to him we just get replacements here. What color size would you like?

Love,
Ma

Celeste wants to know if it is all right for her to every now & then wear some of the cottons you left? She has already, but I told her to get your permission.

Kitchen With Marie Louise's Stove Installed

Letter 10

Postmark 31 Oct 56
Wednesday

Dear Hel

Thanks for your & Neal's card. It must be so much fun to be going around as you are doing. I am glad to hear that Chapel Hill is as good as I have always heard it was. How is Neal doing?

Look -- I have a favor to ask of you. As you know, I try not to interfere in your social life, but I would like you to look up that French boy and if possible to ask him to something. Sometimes you gals are terribly stuffy at your age about accepting someone "different", and I have heard French students at Tulane say how hard it is for them to get dates etc. I'll never forget you & that English friend of Vicki's! I hope this is not too impossible for you to do. For all I know he is very popular & you couldn't get a date with him! Anyway, make an effort to do something for him. Look at it coldly -- you may be in France someday! His name, in case you have not my last letter, is Auguste de Narbonne.

The man is coming around today to see about painting the house. He was here yesterday with your father and I liked his taste. That is, he agreed with mine! I have finally persuaded your father the storm doors should be the front door, and I want the house oyster or putty colored, in no contrasting trim, and the doors black. The man suggested a soft, salty color for the doors, which sounds good, so I think he knows colors. He also said he believed the house was originally the color I want it as it is Victorian Gothic, & they tried in painting to get the look of grey stone gothic. He understands I do not want anything hard, shiny & bright.

Crin's kitty had a terrible convulsion Fri night & your father had to take him to the vets, where he still is. I wish the poor thing would die. I had been very faithful in giving it its two pills a day, but he got the convulsions anyway. He was getting very cute, too. This is I!

Molly feels very much better about Walter being at the Hero's. They told him they had tried out a student last year & had not liked him, and they really wanted one for a baby sitter & he fit the brief. A baby sitter is the last thing I ever thought of Walter being!

Let me know about the French man!

Love, Ma

Letter 11

Postmark 4 pm 5 Nov 56
Monday

Dear Hel

Life is toujours gai. The Dannas had a rip-snorter of a party for Cyn and Lyn, complete with band and dancing in the patio. She had planned it a "two-level" party, with old folks upstairs discussing, presumably, children, schools & servants, and the young downstairs dancing. So who was tearing around downstairs? Natch! No one set foot upstairs. Friday was Butzie's birthday, which she celebrated by having a gay group at that gay function, the

"25 Club", but I managed to squeeze a little fun even out of that. Last night we stayed at the Posey's, just us, and had some of Warren's chinese food -- I have designed them a garden, and am going to go there to measure & plot today. M.L. likes it but I am afraid Warren wants a "professional." This is the plan. [Drawing]. Looks familiar? In the corners will be two lath houses, which I will have to look further into because they are to cover an incinerator and a generator. Herb bed in a spoke pattern around the sundial. Use it or not, it gives me something to do.

I have had a brilliant idea for you to work on. Some time in the spring I feel I'll get itchy feet and thought it would be fun to drive up, pick up 3 or 4 couples of your choosing, & have a house-party at Gap. Afterwards, your father & I could "do" the garden tour, which I have always yearned for. Like it?

Mimi has been chosen cheerleader for Homecoming Game, as all the cheerleaders are in the court.

Pearl has not been here since Halloween night. Can't imagine what has happened. Just one of her periodic spells, I guess, but she usually calls.

Lou is a great deal better. They found she had a bladder infection which was weakening her, and have now cured her of that. She seems cheerful. Took your last letter & read to her, & she is always thrilled about news of you -- being #1, you know.

Love,
Ma

Going to hear V. Borge with Kellys tonight -- Geo. birthday Tuesday [rest blurred by water damage].

Letter 12

Postmark 8:30 pm
5 Nov 56

Dear Hel

Mrs. Boden called today about seeing you etc., and I was delighted to hear from her. Juliana's mother also called, & chatted for a while. Ann seems to have made a hit by writing Julie.

By the way, skip the French boy deal. I thought W. & L. was where Jimmy Bolderick was and that since you wrote he was supposed to have been over to one of your dances, you had perhaps been there. It would really be a very embarrassing thing to do & the guy might wonder about it since he does not know you.

Barney and Molly McCloskey

Crin and Hélène in Kitchen

Leave it alone. His uncle had not mentioned him to me, so there is no reason for you to do anything. He had told Amelie Wogan & she had Alice Howcott write Harley, who already knew him. On second consideration it would be a rather strange thing for you to do. Thanks anyway.

Celeste [Offutt] came down & put her mother in De Paul's, so I hope it will do some good. I had tried Sat, but had no luck.

Love, Ma

Letter 13

Postmark 12 Nov 56
Sunday

Dear Hel

Life is still toujours gai. E. Hayward's daughter's debut party was last Thurs. It was not too large, but quite fun, with band. Had dinner before with the Miles. Geo's birthday party was last Tuesday and by that time it was all Eisenhower, and I was, of course, the odd man out with my Stevenson vote. Your school certainly shows no sign of being a two-party one. In spite of my man not winning I am glad La. went Republican. Saw Bonnie Wisdom in the grocery store couple of days before elections & she asked me to come do some work and I said I was flirting with Stevenson, but if she wanted, I would come help her, but vote for Stevenson, and she almost passed out!

I certainly have inherited poor Va. Kelly. She is so worried about this trip of Vickie's to N.Y. and is trying to plan from here every inch of Vicki's time. I frankly told her I was giving you no instructions and to me it was half the fun for you to do your own planning. Made absolutely no impression. We went to Victor Borge with them Mon. night & she complained constantly thru the performance. She expected a lot of straight piano playing, and as she has absolutely no sense of humor the man left her cold. I do agree it got tiresome. She is upset because Vicki told her I wrote you 3 times a week, and she writes her mother only twice etc. etc. And the money problem!

M.L.'s kitchen is coming along slowly. They are planning to have Xmas dinner there for the family. Lou is at last going home tomorrow. She will be confined to upstairs for some time. She wants [us] to bring over Thanksgiving Dinner but we are afraid it would excite her too much. M.L. got a rumor out that yesterday was Ann's birthday, & Ike came over with a cake, & M.L. with a present. We put the cake in the freezer to save for the 14th

Love, Ma

Your father got a letter from Quin's saying that for $25.00 we could let you ask someone to cast in the ball to be your escort. Would you like to do this?

Neal's mother & Julie's mother both called me last week.

Celeste, Hélène, Crin, Mimi, Warren Posey.
Top Row: Peter Warren Posey, Lou Stauffer, Marie Louise Posey

Letter 14

Postmark 29 Nov 56

Dear Hel

Your letter is wonderful! I am so glad you had Harlequin business, because we were all awaiting anxiously to hear. I went up to Lou's and read it to her & she was beside herself with joy. M.L. loved it. And so did Pearl. We are all doing that repulsive thing known as "living vicariously" or in other words moss on the turtle's back, which is a bad bad simalie? similie? oh you sym -- how the hell!

1213 Third St. Pale Paint

The house is being painted & I made them change the color I loved in a panic, got another, asked them to change to # 1, got a 4th color, had screaming hysterics this morning with 1/2 the house finished, stopped 10 men for 2 hrs. demanded, demanded, demanded <u>all over </u>again -- and then the man, Mr. Geyser, a lovely ascetic type whom M.L. & I are in love with called up <u>so</u> disappointed -- I gave in. It's pale -- I wanted wanted wanted a <u>dark</u> house.

We had a beautiful Thanksgiving dinner but missed dreadfully you, Lou & Celeste, who went over to the Whites. We roasted the wild-rice stuffed turkey on the spit, had mirleton soufflé, salad, and my gorgeous bisquit tortoni liberally laced with brandy -- and what was nicest, <u>no servants.</u> We called Jack McIlhenny to come over, Molly had dinner with us, & Porcher & Martha Miles dropped in & we roared on until 10: Jack's mother, I found out the next day, gave him H double l with an e in the middle. Poor, poor guy. Dreadful Dreadful Stauffer women.

I found M.L. some lovely French Provincial rush bottom side chairs, very delicate fruitwood, browsing about with Lise yesterday and thought they would be lovely for the new kitchen. Took her there today, 3rd floor of a 2nd hand-store & she was wild with joy, but wondered (her words) if "The Bull Moose" would approve, bought them in a fit of defiance. Warren called also beside himself with joy & so grateful to have one detail taken care of & out of the way. I feel proud!

Wild to see you!

Love, Ma

Letter 15

Postmark 4 Dec 56

Dear Hel

I have become reconciled to the color of the house. The blinds will be a slightly darker grey and with the black front door I think it will look very handsome. The men have done a truly beautiful job. One terrible unforeseen by-product was layers of plaster dust filtering on the downstairs floors. I did not realize it was there until Melvin waxed and the whole business created a crystallized mess. Raymond started Sat. on his hand & knees with steel wool and got only the drawing room finished.

Danny & Geo had a cocktail party after the game Sat & then M.L. & Warren went out to dinner with us. Sun Molly & Barney came over & Barney told us all about seeing you on his trip.

I played golf today with Martha & Nelly Page. Did terribly, of course, and could scarcely make the nine holes. It was fun & I think they will let me go next Mon too. My clubs are so rusty & old-fashioned & coming unwrapped.

The young Frenchman's name is de Narbonne Gustave or Auguste, I do not remember which. What class boys do you go out with?

Love, Ma

Letter 16

Postmark 7 Jan 57

Dear Hel

Walter came to tell me good-bye Sat. A very sad occasion. He had weather trouble with the plane yesterday & it was 2 o'clock before he & Pat got off -- & I think missing important connections in the East. Molly & Barney came by in the afternoon for a drink & said Malcolm Monroe was at the air-port to see his daughter off & was in a horribly you know-what condition. A bit of N.O. gossip.

Your father has passed on his bug to Crin and me -- we are however ambulatory cases. She was awake & crying almost all night, so I feel 90 this morning.

I still am reaping compliments thick & fast for you. Butzie Danna said you were not only the best-looking girl at the Howcott's, but also the best dressed. He & Dev are two of your staunchest admirers.

Peg & Walter Simpson had a gala for the Griswold gal. I went with your father, so did not stay long enough to see it reach its climax. I am getting tired of his snatching me home. But, of course, he was feeling still ill.

Mimi was asked to the intellectual group's dinner because, she said, she is failing calculus, and we found a lovely black velvet dress on sale at T & C for her. She said Jacques does not like Harvard because it is anti-intellectual, which puts him at the top of the anti-snob snob list.

Really enjoyed your visit and seeing all your friends.

What do you want us to do about your costume?

Love,
Hélène

Hélène, the 1950's College Student

Letter 17

Postmark 16 Jan 57

Dear Hel

We are all under the weather. Your father is still whooping, I am still whooping, Crin was sick, Ann is whooping and Pearl has not been here this week. As a result, life is very quiet. We went to a debutante dinner that the Dinkins gave for Lyn Hayward, and it was fun, which I did not expect. Most of the debs look so scared and self-conscious. Lyn has a lot more poise and maturity than most. I have also picked a husband for you -- Fritz Jahncke and have put a gris-gris on him so nobody else gets him. Had a long talk with him on the subject of going steady -- which he <u>never</u> has done. He is quite the most attractive of any of the swains I have met this year. We is matchmaking! We are having a lunch on Feb 3 for Lyn & are praying for a warm sunny day. Intend to knock them out with the food -- no warmed over Chez-Vous for me!

I am having a small cocktail party Sat. to pay back a lot of Xmas invitations. Tomorrow I am going to make a fancy paté I just read about in the N.Y. Times.

Please write Jimmy Rogers and thank him for a picture I never sent you. He had the newspaper picture printed & framed as he did the one of your father & me on the

Flandre. His address is

James M. Rogers 1139 Third Street

Celeste made you some cookies last night but they were too salty, so we ate them. I am sending you some from Four Seasons as an Exam treat. Good luck!

> Love,
> Ma

Letter 18

Postmark 22 Jan 57, Jan 15

Dear Hélène:

Sorry you lost your check. Did you lose it without endorsing? Did you endorse it by signing your name on the back. If so it was the same as cash. Did you endorse it "for deposit" to your account. If you didn't endorse it or if you endorsed it for deposit, then it is no good unless your name is forged by someone. Only if you endorsed it simply with your signature was it cash and if you did that it was the same as losing a $50.00 bill. Let me know what you did and if you found it. I'll then do something.

Meanwhile you have some left in the bank. Don't be so careless.

The weather is still nasty and we all still have colds.

>Love,
>>Father

Letter 19

Monday

Dear Hel

Congratulations a million times for the wonderful grade in history. I am very proud of you. Gads -- a brain.

I am sick in bed, but not in bed because Pearl is still sick too. Butzie came by yesterday & gave me a shot of penicillin & some sulfa tablets, so my fever & sore throat have departed, but not the glaring red eyes that make me look like a were-wolf.

We had a humdinger of a party Sat night -- cocktails at 5 which ended at 2 AM. Doesn't seem to matter what time you start, it's always 2 AM. Much dancing etc, and Leeds brought his dinner party over around 11. I was really under the weather but managed to make it until 1 and then went to bed with guests still here. It didn't seem to bother them in the least. Today I had to finish cleaning the drawing room. When you see Fenella, tell her I served the cheese Sat. night & ham that she sent, & everyone wanted to know what kind of cheese it was. I threw away the wrapper and all I remember is that it was a Provolone type, but not who made it. It would be nice if she knew.

I am still carless. Your father said the insurance company has at last given permission to start fixing the car, which will probably take about a week. I find walking very healthy. The blinds still have not dried, the man says. Don't understand why the doors were stripped & back in one day.

Good luck on the exams!

        Love, Ma

Letter 20

Postmark 29 Jan 57

Dear Helene

I wrote the Shumans that you would be in Washington, and I do hope you get a chance to meet them -- the gals are so very delightful and the entire household so much fun. Walter would love them.

Pearl finally came back today after being gone for 2 weeks, so I fled the house & went to see "Baby Doll" -- tell Walter <u>not</u> to miss it -- He will get all the symbolism in the photography that I got plus others I am sure I missed. I would like to discuss it with him. To name a few

1 -- the refinement of the Negro faces
2 -- the hound dog in the hall
3 -- the gal opening the front door & the wind blowing in her face
Plus others

Went to a cocktail party the LeBretons had at the Orleans Club -- found it sticky in spite of the fact they had a band. <u>No one danced</u> except -- guess who -- Donald Halsey. Anyway -- Alvin dragged me off early -- We went with the Miles who like to go early -- Knew no one -- then had to leave as the people started pouring in. Finished up with dinner at Arnaud's.

My party for Lyn is Sunday. I am not afraid as I haven't given a sticky party yet. And I intend to give them something besides warmed over caterers food. There will be 22 in all.

Tell Walter his Granny's wallpaper is simply beautiful in ML's dining room. Newton Howard designed the panels for the wall space & I went Sat & sat with her as the paper hanger hung the paper -- groaning every minute because it was so old & brittle. It took him all day to do 3 small panels & it is perfection! I told her to move the mirror over the mantle & get two simple classic black urns with the reeding for the only decoration & put greens in it and have nothing else as decoration -- nothing on any of the other walls

Give all my love to Fenella --

Hélène

Letter 21

[no envelope, but internal evidence indicates the letter was written between that of 29 Jan and 5 Feb 57]

Dear Hel:

I rented a typewriter for a month, so maybe you will be able to read my letters for a change.

I hate to brag, but the party yesterday was a success fou. We treated the kids to wine and cafe brulot, neither of which they seem ever to have had before, and they were bowled over -- that plus the huge roast, red fish vinaigrette and biscuit tortoni made a meal that they kept coming back for -- plus wild rice and mushrooms. The big French napkins were another source of wonderment, and I made them tie them around their necks. We had all the windows opened, and they loved the fact that without screens they could step out onto the porches and into the garden. Even the swing on the front porch was an unusual feature. I had to make brulot twice. One of the boys told me that if he ever passed this house and saw I was having a party he was coming in, that he had never had so much fun in his life. I also proposed to Fritz Jahncke for you, but he said he would wait for Crin. We played music and everyone danced, and a 1:00 o'clock lunch ended finally at 7. My head is literally swimming with the nice things they said. It is so satisfying to do something for appreciative people.

I can't wait to hear from you all about the Shumans. I hope you love them as much as I do. I do think those girls are a fine bunch, and I am tremendously fond of them, also Polly, who does a wonderful job and has such a good time with them. I envy your seeing them.

I had a disastrous interview with Crin with Mrs. Dreyfus the other day, and it was strictly that woman's fault, and I made no bones about letting her know I thought so. She scared the pants off Crin, firing one question without pause after another, without giving the child a chance to absorb even one. Crin went perfectly willingly into the little separate cubicle with the woman, while I stayed on the outside filling out a form, which will surprise them at some of the unorthodox things I said. However, in two seconds Crin came flying out and stood by my desk, Mrs. D hot behind, firing one question after another at her. She was utterly bewildered, and I told Mrs. D as gently as possible that if she stopped her questions, maybe Crin would get her bearings, but the Jig was up and Crin refused to open her mouth. Mrs. D then began firing questions at me: namely, had Crin ever been to nursery school? No. Why not? I don't approve of them. Which floored her. Then I explained my theory that what I did gave Crin great independence, and I have found that cooperation came later, but independence and an ability to play by herself were to me vastly important etc.etc.etc. I am convinced the woman had some place to go, because she wanted me to go thru the lower school, and after I had gotten Crin to follow us outside with the greatest of difficulty, she (Mrs. D) dashed across the street and spoke to two 6 yrs. olds and dashed back to me and said they would take me thru the school. Crin refused to cross the street, even with the enticement of being able to play on the swings, so I started with her to my car, as Mrs. D started for hers. So she said "Aren't you going thru the school", and I said "No", so she dashed over again and told the 6 yrs olds not to wait, got in her car and left. The very interesting fact to me in this whole business is that my interview was at 10:30, and counting traveling time I was home by 5 to 11! Nuts on interviews! Miss Devlin called me today, and I spoke very frankly to her about it all. She has another next week, but I bet I will not be able to drag her there. They say "Prepare that child for what to expect", and I said I had told her she was going to school to take a test, but what on earth does that mean to a child who has had no experience with which to draw on. I also asked Miss Devlin if it was done purposely in that way in order to weed out the "sensitive". She denied that, and said all but 2 of the children had been able to respond. I told her of the time angle, and said I suspected Mrs. D. had some place to go, but she also denied that. I hope that Miss Aiken makes a place for Crin. She herself said she would rather go there, naturally, after the other day.

M.L. and Warren have a wonderful trip to Chicago for a week. I told you their kitchen is finished, all except for the stainless steel on the sink, and it is lovely. The floors got stained a beautiful color, and they are waiting for the living room to dry before the curtains go up. I wrote you how perfectly gorgeous the dining room murals were, didn't I? Such classicism! Gads, how I rave, but it really is all of that and more.

How did you do on your exams?

Love and kisses, Ma.

Letter 22

Postmark 5 Feb 57

Dear Hel

So good to hear from you. We tried telephoning, but as we did not remember the name of your dorm, the school could not get in touch with you. An amoeba among other amoebas! Your description of your room makes it sound as if you are living the ascetic, scholarly life of a Middle Age nun.

Ham Hall came to town with his son Doug and I put on a party for him that lasted until 2:30, and I got to the family-attacking stage, this time on Walter. Molly & Barney left pretty early, as did Poch & Martha, but M.L. and Warren stuck it through, as did Cyn and Ham. I made a really lovely center-piece of green grapes only in an epergne that was much admired. The mousse was not very good; I had made it too fast and did not squash the black-berries enough. The roast was good, as always, and Cyn contributed a perfectly delicious Tenn. ham, and we had the Moselle. Ham did not get passed out; behaved beautifully. Doug is quite good-looking, alert and intelligent, blond like his mother, English-looking, but Celeste says he is pretty conceited. He took her out the next night, and called Mimi to go to a frat party but she was already going to one.

I had my first board meeting yesterday, and got through it o.k., in spite of the fights, which I found made me still want to giggle helplessly in front of them all while they argued if the CURTAIN TIME PARTY should be at the Pont[chartrain Hotel]. or the St. Charles and whether the dinner should be tax-deductible and tip or tax deductible without tip, or just the tip and not tax deductible, and there were two women on the floor which is against all parliamentary procedure, and others interrupting, and Leone Rothschild trying to be recognized legitimately, and someone making a motion, and another making a motion before the first motion was voted on, and when I corrected her, saying she was making an amendment to the motion, which had not been yet voted on, and this was the day the Parliamentarian hadn't come & I was counting on her and so did not bring my Robert's Rules of Order. I was waving my hands and really giggling, but Leone got furious, when I leaned over and said Just interrupt, everyone else is, and just GLARED at me, so I BANGED with the gavel and yelled in my best voice, which seems to command immediate attention, and said Mrs. Rothschild wants to ask a question, which was wrong as Mrs. R. knows all the answers, so she said I Do Not, I Want To Say Something. Well the next one was when Mrs. Morgan Whitney said, well, she didn't see why they sold records at the Book Fair, they were all broken by the time they were unpacked from the paper cartons, and Joan May, chairman of last year's Book Fair, said WELL, MRS. WHITNEY, I just wish you would tell us how to pack records! etc.etc. so, when she finished, I mildly said, well, I broke my record the minute I bought it, does that mean anything?

However, I had called all the ladies the day before and asked them to prepare SHORT reports, and in spite of the fact of old hands like Janet Yancey, etc. predicting a LONG

49

meeting, and that she was sorry, but that she would have to leave at 12, I had the meeting started and going at 11:45, and when the clock struck 12 and the bells of the Jesuit Church peeled, the meeting was OVER, and Martha came dashing up the very first up front and gave me the MOST HEARTY congratulations, and two or three people called and said it was a very enthusiastic meeting and good and Martha called today and said, Helene, you can really do it, you need not be afraid again, and told me how she had seen people just fall flat on their behinds with fear when they were in the Chairman's chair.

I am trying to write this with Ann on the bed screaming can I oh mother can I go out to susanmaryjones on sat, and Crin mother, oh mother where oh where is my red balloon and can I have a piece of paper and your father has anyone seen my kit of red tools, has anyone seen my kit of red tools, has anyone seen my kit of red tools, and Mimi is modeling her new suit complete with blouse, shoes etc.

Yours in confusion, Ma

Letter 23

Postmark 14 Feb 57

Dear Helene

I am terrifically proud of you and your really wonderful grades on your examinations. Your father wants me to take them to Mrs. Schultz and show them to her, which I'll do tomorrow. The purpose of that is to show how very anxious we are to have Celeste and Ann in the next term.

Crin and Ann in Mardi Gras Finery

I took Crin for another test at Newman, and this time it went better. I asked Miss Devlin to be there, as I know she has a softer approach, and it worked. However, that old goat, Miss Dreyfus, said she could not give Crin a complete test, because what she did not want to answer she simply did not answer, and she recommended highly that the child be sent to nursery school. I merely laughed. I will know if she is accepted some time next week. Miss Aiken cannot give me an answer about Crin; she can get in primer, but would have to be put out of the first grade, which would leave us high and dry. Oh, well, maybe she will have to be sent to McDonough # whatever it was that your father has such fond memories of.

My conference with Ann's teacher was one of joy. She said Ann had improved more than anyone in the class (maybe there was more need!) that her grades were excellent and she had pulled herself up from the middle to one of the top students. Ann was very anxious to know what her deportment grade was, and it was A. Apparently she has been making quite an effort not to talk.

Your father has planned a trip for Sunday. We are taking the train to Baton Rouge, because Ann and Crin have never been on a train before, go see the Capitol, and come back that afternoon. Ann is also asking Beth and everyone is in a high state of excitement, including me. No hamburgers to fix. Of course, your father is talking the usual "picnic lunch", the cheapskate, but I am turning a very deaf ear. Gads, getting on the train with numerous boxes does not appeal to me at all. I like restaurants!

I am in another state of excitement. I wrote a critical analysis of the movie "Baby Doll", and sent it to the "New Yorker", and for the second time in my life I am on probation. I have passed the first test; they sent me another letter saying that they like it very much and had sent it on to the editors concerned. The first time that happened, the editors concerned let my piece die a natural death, so this time I am praying and hoping and keeping my fingers crossed, and awaiting the mail-man with feverish anxiety. I have Lise sending the proper thought-waves on to N.Y., and Cynthia concentrating because of my friends I feel that those two would really be delighted. It is an impossibility, I know, but a gal can dream, can't she?

I went to hear Sir Thomas Beecham last night and it was thrilling. I feel very proud, that knowing nothing whatever about music I could definitely hear last night that that man was literally pulling sounds from our local orchestra that I had never heard them produce before. I could not possibly express it in musical terms, and when I read the criticisms in the papers today, it was all properly expressed.

      Love, Ma.

Letter 24

7

What a life you are leading! Chapel Hill must have been marvelous.

Went with Lise to hear the great cellist, Piaigorsky, and it was the first time I have ever heard a cello as a solo instrument. The last piece call "Schelomo" by Bloch, a Hebrew Rhapsody, had me sitting there with tears pouring down my cheeks, and me with no handkerchief, as usual. I had to blot myself with my gloves, and then wring the gloves out. Lise took me down afterwards to meet the man, and before I knew what I was saying I told him that my compliment to him was my red eyes, and he gave my hand a wonderful squeeze. So I was in a 16-year old daze all the time Lise and I were having coffee at the French Market afterwards, much to her amusement.

Went last night to hear a lecture by John Mason Brown, and among the things he said was that Shaw said he always played Mozart while he was writing, so I have the proper instincts for a writer, anyway, as I sit up-stairs at the rented typewriter with the music bellowing downstairs in the drawing-room, and have to dash down every 10 or so minutes to turn the record over. Your father is giving me quizzical looks over his glasses when he thinks I am not looking; his patience is truly unlimited. However, I got blown, but good, this morning when he discovered the same two shirts with the same two buttons missing that had been missing for a month. So, I sew. I don't know if I told you that I decided to try to write a story. It has the old Delord-Sarpy house and our old house in it, and I have done a lot of research at the library, and spent days tramping over the old Sarpy house, which is being torn down to make way for the bridge. I have a good idea, but the inability to express myself is driving me slightly nuts. I hastily wrote a rough draft and sent it to Dorothy Ricciutti for criticism. She was -- kind. Said I had some good things in it, but it was under-developed, and suggested a course in Creative Writing at Newcomb. But Mr. Shaw said he avoided English teachers all his life, and attributes his success to that. If I compare myself to anyone, it is the best, brother! It is in my desk, and every now and then I take it out and scratch and fumble among the feeble brains and write some more. I aim for the New Yorker; no fun to try unless it is hard to get into. They have never let me know anything about that criticism, so I guess they let it die, again. Wish they would send it back, because I would try somewhere else. I don't know the proper etiquette and if two weeks is time enough to be on the ropes, groggy.

Ann caught me taking a peep at Mrs. Kirby's intended as he came for her yesterday morning, and fussed at me for spying on my neighbors. It was hard to defend myself, and one thing lead to another and she ended up with a very astute remark: that Mrs. Maunsell was the kind who would pull her windows down before she screamed!

Mimi is having that cute girl from Birmingham, whatever her name is, for Carnival, and Barney got them call-outs to Mystic, which should make the trip for her. The way I fuss and fume about Mystic, he should not be so kind. However, this year I look forward to it, because I know that gal will have her eyes popping.

Va. Penick is in town and came over the other afternoon and when we ran out of bourbon we started in on the scotch and were at the screeching stage when your father and Ike arrived at 5. Just took one hour. Both enjoyed it thoroughly. She said the Dean of Women [at Randolph-Macon], I thinking the Dean, was one of her best friends at Wellesley, and why-by-God hadn't I written her that you were at R.M. Also, Al has countless relatives in Lynchburg who would love to have you over, and she is going to see about it. I should not desert my old friends.

Love, Ma.

(over)

Hélène, Mimi, Hélène, Alvin at the Gap 1957

I still haven't given up entirely about the house-party. If not at spring vacation, why not a week-end after? I know it might be cruel to make your father do all that driving, because he does not, rightly, trust me with the wheel, but I would love to go see the Va. gardens after the house party. Would you fly home for spring vacation? I am still sissy about going to Gap with all of you in the summer; it is too much work. However, 8 and 18 makes a slight difference.

Letter 25

Postmark 27 Feb 57

Dear Hel

I would be delighted to have Ann come home with you, and have written her mother to that effect. I hope she will, it would be fun to have her.

Oberon the other night was a great deal of fun as it always is. I saw the Carrere girl on the dance floor and introduced myself to her. Her dress was one of prettiest in the ball. I told her to tell you hello for me. After the ball, Lise, M.L., Molly, Dot Ricciutti and the respective men went for oysters and beer at Delmonico's, and afterwards we had a night-cap at Lise's adorable house in St. Louis St., and she played the piano and sang for us. Bill and Warren were completely bowled over by Lise's charm, and at the ball she had one of those mystery dances that make a ball fun, even when one is middle-aged. She was thrilled.

Celeste went completely overboard the past weekend for the entire crew of a Belgium sailing vessel that was in port for a week. The boys were mostly Flemish, and Valencia had parties Friday, Saturday and Sunday for them. She was invited to go on the ship Monday afternoon, so I got soft-hearted and got her excused from gym so she could go. Myself, I think there is nothing like a European man! Apparently, so does Celeste. Anyhow, Monday at 5 she and three of her breathless friends arrive home from the ship, and I am informed that 4 of the boys are to come here for dinner; all I had to do was supply the house, one of the mothers had already cooked some chicken and made some potato salad. At 6:45 I went downstairs, already in my pink ball gown, because they were expected at 7 and I was expecting my friends at 7:30 for a pre-ball drink, when one of the little fools comes pussyfooting in just as I was pouring myself a necessary first drink, after having set the table with candles and my best salt-sellers, and informs me I had to go to the docks and pick up the boys as her mother had changed her mind about going for them. I rip out with the blue, put the drink down, grab my stole and two of the little jackasses, and off we go to the docks. We wait, we wait and we wait, these two little femmes de navy meanwhile having much chat with many of these cute characters on board. Of course, they did not know the last names of the 4 we were to pick up, just Jean, Jacques etc. etc. We were assured and re-assured that just one minute, they were coming. 45 minutes later, me getting madder and madder, two of the tiniest little scared rabbits show; honestly, they looked about Ann's age. So cute, so shy, so adorable in their navy blues, so polite, so reassuring that JUST ONE MINUTE MORE and their two companions would be off. My high-heel clad feet have long since becoming unfeeling lumps, and the stole is not much protection from the wind that whips from the river. I finally just plain lose my temper. Other children, I find, do not seem concerned about listening: I had said five times I was expecting company, had to get to a ball etc. everyone so sympathetic, but JUST ONE MINUTE MORE! It took a few blasts from my fog horn voice and a few stamps of the feet to convince Celeste's friends that when I said go, I meant it. Having once given way, I pour out with non-consideration of the young, that they made nuts of themselves hanging around ships, where was their pride, etc.etc., in front of these adorable polite little Belgians. Anyway, we get home with two of the prize packages anyway. My friends were already here in the green room, and Harry Belafonte was holding forth in the drawing-room with Celeste and the other gal. After a drink, I went into apologize to the boys, but they were so surrounded and looked so happy and the gals were practically lighting their cigarettes for them that I sneaked out. Molly said reassuringly that they probably have mothers who scream, too. My last glimpse of them was through the porch window, and they were on the large red sofa, plates of food on their laps, and the gals at their feet on the floor.

Red Sofa in the Drawing Room With Rented Piano, Sèvres Urn and Boulle Cabinet in Background

We get to the ball, and I find that somewhere between Lise's house and the Auditorium I have made way with my call-out. I leap out of the car while it is still moving, thinking that it maybe is in my lap, Barney meanwhile trying to grab me thinking in my agitation I am doing away with myself. Malcolm Monroe sees this fool thing, comes up and inquires the trouble. When I tell him, he says for a kiss, he'll get me in, so I says, cheap at the price, and if anyone can get me in a Ball without a call-out it is a Monroe. So he says, take my arm and I take his arm, and we get to the door and Malcolm looks straight ahead and says in a stern voice, I, personally, will vouch for this woman, and we march in before the man even knows what we had done. Marie Louise was right behind us, and she said when the man finally realized, his agitation knew no bounds, that he kept muttering, I can't let that man get away with that; however, I head to the call-out section, and when the man at the door there put his hand out for the card, I took it and shook it and said, it's been so long since I have seen you; that threw him and by the time he recovered, I was on the front row.

Mystic, Saturday, will be more proper!

        Love, Ma.

Letter 26

Postmark 6 Mar 57

Dear Hel

I hope I have not been deserting you; I seem to be in a sort of a kind of daze, since Friday, really. Friday night Lise Todd had a party for Va. and Al Penick. She said come at parade time, which means 7 to me, so we arrive and find her in her shift -- the parades pass on Royal at 8:30! So Alvin and I tramp Canal Street, which I had not done in years, had a drink at the St. Charles bar, watched the parade there and on Royal Street both, and make the party at the proper time. We left early, as we were both rather tired from the long walks. The next night was Mystic. Mimi's guest arrived at the airport that afternoon; it was supposed to have been morning, so we had lunch and waited the three hours that the plane was late. I think Patsy had a treat seeing Mystic, and she had an anonymous dancer ask her for a dance, which always adds to the thrill. We went afterwards for oysters and beer, and then to M.L. and Warren's for a nightcap, and then home. The next night the Danna's had a cocktail party for the Penick's and her sister Marjorie, which was a humdinger, but we left early again. Mimi had given me instructions not to come home tight. While we were still at the party, she frantically telephones that Crin has the measles; I had discovered the fact just as we were leaving the house, but just did not mention it, thinking she would not really pop out until the next day. Monday Crin was rather under the weather, and Celeste was wonderful to her, reading to her and cutting out paper dolls and playing the phonograph for her all day. That night, Al and Va. came over and had ducks and wild rice and wine with us. Yesterday, your Father went to the Danna's by himself. Ann spent the day with a friend, and Crin and I spent the day here. His costume, I hear, made a hit. He had none, but as he left the house, picked a sprig of ivy and pinned it on the back of his trousers. Natch!

Last night, we went to the Hopkins' party-after-Comus. As we are not invited to Comus, it was rather a struggle to keep awake until 12 to start out. I had not been to their house in years, and simply did not know anyone there. However, several people seemed to know me, and it worked out to be very pleasant and rather quiet. Nobody, really, had much pep left Carnival night. Their house is old and shabby and unpainted and it was filled with the old

Celeste, Mimi and Hélène 1957

type Creole sitting in chairs, young people, and children in night-gowns peeping over the banisters; a party full of character. Their specialty is Cherries which have been soaking all year in brandy, and a couple of that nice fruit puts you in the mood for gayety.

Last week I stopped on Canal St. and had sent to you one of those Carnival newspapers that really don't show a thing, but I thought you might enjoy getting it. I hope it wasn't a jip. Did you get the pralines from Solari's?

Love, Ma

Letter 27

Postmark 12 Mar 57

Dear Hel

The typewriter was overdue for so long that I rented it for another month, so you can have peace for a little longer. Your get-well card came, and Crin was so thrilled to have something of her own to open. She is all well now, and all I have to wait for is Ann to come down with it.

Today I was supposed to be "cookie Mother" for the Brownie troupe; someone had called me last Thursday just as I was to leave for a lunch at Brennan's, and I accepted and of course promptly forgot about it. Today, I leisurely went to market, to Weeze's, and then back home at about 3:15, and was making a cup of coffee in the kitchen, when Pearl tells me of the disaster. The Devil had me by the tail, because I was dripping my first cup of coffee of the day, as Mimi had drunk up all the coffee the night before, and I was really all prepared to sit and listen to some music and drink my coffee. I dripped one more dripper and then my Guardian Angel took me by the hand and made me go to the grocery store and buy up the gooiest, marshmallowest bunch of cookies as I could find and go to the meeting. I got there as Ann was passing a large tray of cookies, so I pretended I was a man on the float and said "Catch", and when the gals saw the gooie kinds they went wild. They ate them all up. I got also a cup of coffee, because Jane took me in the kitchen and lo and behold there was a large pot sitting on the most beautiful antique gas stove with ten burners you ever saw. So virtue pays. Ann just told me that the gals told her that I was the best cookie Mother they ever had! Gee, I feel good, now.

Did I tell you that I am trying to learn French? Your father got me some of those Living Language records, and I have, in the first flush of enthusiasm, been listening about two hours a day. So far, the lessons are easy, and I keep going over and over the easy ones because I don't want to use my brain on the hard ones. What a struggle it is to try and concentrate. I have discovered a fool proof method of getting the pronunciation down. I shall pass it on to you, because your accent stinks. Of course, you have to have the records to follow the man, so you can do this when you get home. However, you really can do it anytime. It is this: put your finger over your lips as if you are saying "Shh", keep it there tightly and you will be forced to use the important throat muscles, and the sound will be forced through the nose, to give that slightly nasal quality that French has. My throat is as sore as it can be after doing this for three days two hours a day, but I guarantee I can swing a mean rrrrr and the notes of the sounds are more fully rounded. Gee, I love it when I say Paul. I figured this out, because I remember watching Frenchmen speak and saw that they kept their lips almost closed when they talked, and I remember wondering about it. Keep this a secret, because I shall patent it and make a fortune showing people how to speak perfect French.

We had two parties the past week-end. One was a farewell party for the Swedish Psychiatrist and his wife who have been to Tulane for a year. As it was the first time I had been to this house I talked to myself all the way over there as to how I was going to behave in a very quiet manner, and sit down and not talk too much. Soo --- I meet a very attractive half-Englishman, half Irish-man, keep him pinned until I have the entire story of his life, which is fascinating, and give him the entire story of my life, not so; then I tell the host there is only one thing wrong with the lovely party and that I am going to be rude enough to tell him. He turns pale for half a second until I say there is no music, so with alacrity he puts on Belafonte, and asks me to dance. Well, I take off like a flying saucer with a few low down hip shakes, and the poor man turns pale and runs literally. So I stand in the middle of the floor and am really hurt, until the big Swede comes to my rescue. So I say, Oh a stiff European dancer, and try to teach him to swing <u>his</u> hips. So your father snatches me home and tells me how I have disgraced myself and him, too. Well, it was just doing what we do over here, at Weeze's and Molly's and it just never, never occurred to me someone would be shocked. I was merely trying to be funny. Hereafter, I shall waltz to Belafonte.

Yesterday, we went to Gin Carley's for a wonderful meal that her Lebanese mother cooked for us; so many exciting things to eat, including raw meat balls, tiny, tiny hors d'oeuvres, things rolled up in grape leaves, marvelous meat pies in a kind of bread instead of pastry, and everything so gently seasoned and un-greasy that you could eat and eat and never have even the slightest touch of distress. Everyone was at home with everyone else and when Margie Kehoe took off with an imitation of a strip teaser's bumps and grinds, we were rolling on the floor with glee. As your father said, she was reared with a phonograph. She could make her living doing it with no trouble. The climax was when she made her mother get up on the floor with her and do them too. If you could have seen this stout, lovely-looking white haired, blue eyed woman doing a twin bump-and-grind with her daughter you would not have believed your eyes. What fun!

This week is tres gai. Friday, the Ricciutti's are having their first open house, Saturday I am having a Garden-District Party (I am trying to crash "SOCIETY") and

Sunday a cocktail party that Peggy Dupree is having. You remember, she was the one who had that dreadful sleeping sickness, recovered, was bedridden for a long time, and is now able to get about in a wheel-chair a-la-Marjorie Lawrence. Such courage. Her speech is very thick and slow, but her brain is as quick as it always was, and you can see by the alertness of her eyes that she is taking everything in.

It is really a struggle to sit here and try to write; Crin is at my elbow with white shoe polish spilling on the newly waxed floor; Ann is bouncing Celeste's volley ball right behind my head; Celeste and your father are indulging in the usual squabble about not ordering something from the drug store; the telephone is ringing and no one will answer it (gee, I miss you) and I am trying to concentrate! Gads, and they wonder why I break out with the Confederate Yell quite frequently!

Love, Ma

Letter 28

Postmark 19 Mar 57

Dear Hel

To escape. We had a cocktail party Saturday night with the "Garbage District" crowd and knocked their eyes out. I also mixed in a few other people that I liked and knew would stay late. Knowing the social set, I knew that they would come, have a couple of drinks, and then leave, which is just what happened. It was the first time I had the Howcotts, Strachans, Simpsons etc.etc., and I really floored them with the candles in the drawing room and the food in the dining-room. Peggy called yesterday and said Harley said the drawing room was the most elegant looking room he had ever been in, that there was not one piece of furniture in it that was not good. Rose had walked thru the back gate and liked tremendously what I had done to the garden; the last time she was here was when Crin was a baby and I had the crib in the dining-room, and she raved about the house, too. Someone else said that she thought this was really the most beautiful house in the city, and she had driven a crowd of out-of-town doctors past it to show that she knew the best. Mrs. Wilson said that her husband would want to bring his architectural students through it. Well, I am in a daze.

We had the most terrific accident in the dining-room just as the party was getting under way. I had a smoked turkey, fish vinaigrette, crawfish on toothpicks stuck in a pineapple with drawn sauce, daube glacé, and had borrowed M.L.'s silver vegetable dish with alcohol burner like mine to have two dishes of welsh rarebit. Well, the heat made the beer in the rarebit catch on fire, there was almost an explosion, and the finish I had spent all last summer, practically, putting on the table was gone in a flash. I managed to salvage one rarebit from the two by taking it to the kitchen and stirring in some more beer, and in spite of the slightly scorched taste Dorothy Ricciutti asked for the recipe. However, it undid me for a few seconds. The party lasted until two, with everyone sitting on the floor and listening to music by candlelight. I really think it was a wonderful party.

The night before, we had gone to the Ricciutti's open house, and their new house is a tremendously exciting place, very modern, but two-storied with an enormous roof and a huge glass room up-stairs that looks out on the lake. Downstairs is a tremendous terrace that I really can't explain how you get to except to say that I felt like Alice melting through the looking-glass, and there I was, outside. It was a beautiful night, with one of those round, red moons and if they had had it especially hung for a stage effect it could not have been more perfect. After that, we dropped in on the Haywards, who had asked us to dinner, but I could not accept because the R's, but we went because there was an old friend of mine in for the doctor's convention she wanted me to see. It was about nine, but they had not yet had dinner, so I sat on the sofa with Perry Thomas who had not seen me in 15 yrs. and just held my hand and said "Why, Helene, Why Helene" until I got rather embarrassed, and then brought up the time he had taken me to a medical frat party. Well, I disgraced myself in your father's eyes, because I was sitting on this slippery little Louis Quinze sofa with a silk dress on talking with my arms as usual, and I suddenly found myself on the floor. Everyone sprang to the rescue, but I announced I liked sitting on the floor, and made Perry and Gordon sit with me. Dinner was announced, and Liz insisted that we bring our drinks to the dining-room, over your father's protests, because he was now convinced that I was squiffed (I think he was annoyed by Perry), but I went in the dining-room and me eyes bulged. There was this enormous table all set for 20 with Bohemian glass and the wrapped wine bottles and lobsters kicking on their tails on the sideboard, so I grabbed a plate and said I was staying, after all. After all, it was what Liz had begged and begged us to do when she invited us. Your father and Barney stood by the door with embarrassment all over their foolish faces, so of course, we left. He said I had humiliated everyone and kept them from having dinner. Ah me! Sooooooo, we went to an elegant joint, you know, on Magazine street and had raw oysters instead of lobsters, and beer instead of wine.

Ann is gradually getting over the measles. She is miserable because she can't read. The cat took a chunk out of Crin's arm, but she was dragging him up the steps by his stomach, so wouldn't you?

We went to Peggy Dupree's party; and I almost hate to write about it. Peg Simpson had called to see that we got there at the same time, because she wouldn't know anyone, you know that attitude. She made me furious. The place was decorated with crepe-paper twisted from the corners to the chandeliers in the middle, and of course, we knew no-one. It was a St. Patrick's day celebration, given by Peggy D's sister. It was so sad. And Peg S. kept talking about the crepe paper and whispering about the people until I got sick at my stomach. Peggy D sat in her wheelchair in the front room, and all the old Irish relatives sat around the room on chairs pushed against the wall. Believe me, I put on my happiest, gayest manner, and made good friends with three of Peggy D's cousins, who were most attractive women, and we talked about Europe and they were most gay and intelligent and funny, as the Irish are. Walter S looked so uncomfortable he looked sick, and when I told him to take a deep breath and relax he shot me a look that should have killed, but believe me didn't.

Well, Lent is here, but as the Englishman at my party said, what difference does it make here?

Did I tell you that Mary Casey is in town to buy up English Antique furniture to take back to England!!!!!!!! Ike is having a dinner party at Antoine's for her Wednesday.

Can't wait, can't wait, can't wait to see you. I am so sorry Ann is not coming with you. Anyone else?

    Love,
      Ma

Letter 29

Postmark 25 Mar 57

Dear Hel

Thanks oodles for the wonderful anniversary card. Nice to get it a week ahead! It's the 28th, you know. It reminded me of it, however; and Pops, too.

We had a perfectly fabulous time Saturday night with the Nicholas Oliviers. It was his birthday, and the celebration could not have been other than perfect after he delivered personally a large manilla envelope containing the cleverest invitation I have ever seen. It was a montage of ads he had cut out of the New Yorker and photostated; all of this trouble for 6 people. We went first to their house for cocktails, then to Antoine's in the back most private room, the one that is only truly private because no one can come tramping through. The minute I saw three wine glasses on the table, I knew the dinner would be excellent, and it was: vichyssoise, pompano Pontchartrain, ending with crepe suzettes aflame, to which I started singing Happy Birthday and everyone joined in. We went afterwards back to the house, where he had a magnum of Champagne icing on the coffee table. Perfection is hard to attain, but this was it. He also did something that touched me terrifically; before I left, he handed me a package and would not let me open it. When I got home, I found it was a completely out-of-print and unobtainable collection of Creole Negro stories, written in their own version of the French language, with an English translation of each story. I am truly thrilled, and phoned Betty the next day to see if he truly wanted to give it to me, that I understood those feelings of generosity after being softened up by good food and wine, and that I would be happy to read it and return it, but she insisted he wanted me to have it. I consider it a very valuable addition to my small library.

We got home for a shocker. Celeste had in the beginning of the week asked me if she could have a slumber party, with boys over before hand. I had said no, not once but the dozen of times that she kept asking, because we were going out. She had flounced out of the room in a rage saying, well, then, she just wouldn't have the party. Friday at 5 she comes to me for $5 for her slumber party. I give it to her, thinking she had decided after all to have just girls. As we were leaving the house for dinner she tells me that 2, two, mind you, deux, boys had said at school that they were coming over, so I said I guess it would make you a stinker if you had said no, so at the last minute I asked Pearl to stay. At 12:30 we drove up, the joint was rocking. Harry Belafonte had never played it so loud. Every light ablaze top to toe. All the windows open. I heard someone give a warning, and when I walked thru the drawing room window the first thing I saw was no top on the Sèvres Jug, a broom against the door and something swept under the broom. I scream, but Celeste appears with a mop in her hand, dying cow look in the eyes, and said she had taken them both off for safekeeping. Popcorn, peanuts, cookies and junk ground into the Oriental. Everyone sitting down, still as still with innocent looks on their foolish faces. So I ask loudly what they had been up to before I walked in; and then I say to Celeste to introduce me to her friends, and she doesn't know half their names and I have to introduce myself. So I turn off the phonograph and say there is such a thing as it being 12:30, such a thing as Alvin and I wanting to go to sleep, so the party is over and for the hulking boys to come back tomorrow and clean the place up, which was greeted with howls of mirth, the dogs! I was and am truly annoyed. I do not like parties here when I am not here, but you know Celeste. If it is what she wants, she'll have it. The first one of you to absolutely disregard what I say. Pearl was sitting like a fat Buddha upstairs, looking quietly at television. However, she is no match for a situation like this. The next morning I found throw-up on the side porch, beer cans strung all across the front of the sidewalk, and that they had amused themselves also by tearing up a telephone book and wiping their feet on the white woodwork. All the sexy little gals said it was a SIMPLY WONDERFUL PARTY, MRS. HERO. No doubt, no doubt.

Today, Lise and I went to the rehearsal of the Symphony. We are having two artists tonight: a pianist, Kintner, and Virgil Thomas, who is conducting his own symphony, so it was a double header. She goes often, but this was the first time I had ever been, and it was a great treat. Also, Lise had brought in a paper bag our lunch, including with it some white wine and wine glasses, so we sat upstairs in style and great enjoyment. It is a revelation to see these men relaxed, or rather, working, with their hair down, and not in the stiff, formal way you see them when they perform. Also, I am beginning to actually be able to hear music; Lise is a good teacher, and before she gets through with me I might have learned something. So now I have to stop to get dressed to go to the performance.

Love, M.

I forgot to say that your father had a perfect brain-storm of a present to give Nick: a solid gold tooth pick!

Letter 30

Postmark 11 Apr 57

The table's down to $495. Am still holding out!

Dear Hel   Wed.

Madeline's party was very huge and very good Sunday. She did a queer thing, however -- all the curtains were drawn, candles & lights lit & she received in a black dinner dress! This at 12:30! The food & drinks were excellent, and she had some people from N. Hampshire who were interesting to talk to.

I don't know how I got through Monday. Effel had cocktails at 11, I did marketing for my party at 10:30, lunch with Alice at 12 at the Pontchartrain, home for 2:30, set the table outside for the 12 who were coming here, and it immediately poured down rain. I was too tired to do anything about it, so left for a meeting at Martha Lyons' about the Symphony with Lise. Find myself being suddenly called part of the "executive" committee to recruit younger women in the service of the symphony. Plenty of hard-faced perennial club women types sitting around, with their brains audibly ticking. Left feeling immensely dumb, but Lise says we can be useful by supplying "enthusiasm".

The dinner was good, in spite of the fact that after the rains the temperature dropped 20* and we all sat outside all bundled up to eat. One result was heartened appetites -- they cleaned me out of food in 10 minutes. It made me feel that I had under bought. We ate dessert inside, as we were all icicles by that time. There was much dancing afterwards with Garrett putting on the best performance I have ever seen. I literally rolled on the floor with laughter. The man has no bones. He said Barbara & Al were really having the best time they had had in N.O. & I hope so.

Last night Lise, Cyn & I went to the Symphony on board the "President" a pops concert, and it was very good. Much fun cruising down to Walnut Street and back & strolling on the deck listening to the music.

Tonight I am home & it is driving me screwy having to talk to Crin every 5 min. The television man came to "fix" the television & it did its usual -- died 5 minutes after it was finished being fixed.

Emmy called & said she was coming over. Hope so.

Love, Hel

PS Pops is getting me a portable.

Letter 31

Postmark 14 April 57

Dear Hel

Hooray! Pops bought this cutest of cute typewriters for me; a second-hand Hermes, so you will no longer have trouble reading what I write. It rather sticks on certain letters, but what does that matter.

I am thrilled beyond measure because I found a graduation dress for Mimi for only $24.00 at Gus Mayer's, and it is really lovely. White organdy with narrow tucks, horizontal, the only trimming, and a wide band of plain organdy on the bottom of the skirt and a midriff of plain organdy, scoop neck and short tight sleeves. The skirt is not too full, which she wanted. It is slightly shop-worn, but a trip to Raffo will fix that up. The single-spacing goes double and your father is furious with me because the day he brought it home I was tired and refused to try it out. I could not get a job as a stenographer, could I?

The trip to Harvard sounds thrilling and I am delighted you are getting a chance to see about my most favorite section of the country. Lucky you.

I got the dining-room table for $400 and if I had had the courage to do what George suggested I might have got it for less. He suggested writing out a check for $350, and giving it to her; said none of those stores could resist cash in hand, and as a matter of fact, when she accepted my offer she said she would if I made it cash. Well, I needn't be piggish, but it does kill me not to have found a bargain on Magazine street as I usually do. I am now faced with the almost impossible problem of trying to sell my old one. Bland and Corinne had so very many nice things to say about you; that you were not only very pretty, but as nice as you were pretty.

I also found a terrific bargain for myself at Holmes, where I had gone to see if there were any of the bridal gowns left over, which there weren't. It is a crushed strawberry color peau de soie with a long tight skirt, Empire waist swathed in chiffon that ties high in the back and forms long panels, long tight sleeves, and a wide V neck. It was half-price. Gads, I am so glad most women in N.O. don't like simple clothes, it enables me to get them for almost nothing at the end of the season.

Your floor has been painted and the room looks so cute and bright I want to move back there myself. Raymond painted the wood part of the porch chairs black, but I don't know if it is successful or not. I think to have some yellow, pale cushions made because I now find the effect rather funereal.

We are at home the entire week-end and it is truly nice for a change not to be out gadding. The weather has been super-super, chilly and clear. The bugs are eating the roses, and the white fly the orange trees, so Raymond did some spraying today. The Shasta daisies are about to bloom between the azalea bushes, so the garden may start having a little spot of color, although I do like it all green.

Love, Ma

Hélène's Bedroom

Letter 32

Postmark 18 Apr 57

Dear Hel

The typewriter was short-lived. Your father took it back to see if they could fix the defects and they just tried to sell him a new one -- a $50.00 come-on! I am distressed; so, I imagine are you.

Did you buy a charm at Hausmann's for $8.50? We got a bill & I can't imagine what for. I mean I know I didn't.

Emmy came over to see me yesterday & we had a good long talk. I hope it helped her, she seemed quite distressed over fights with her mother. The gal seems to be working it out and I told her I thought it wonderful that she is reaching maturity at an early age.

Your father keeps talking about trips & things. He really wants to go to Nicaragua, but I have that terrible phobia about flying together that I do not seem able get over. He brought home maps of a trip to Va. & it looks so long & far away & I know he is tired & needs a rest. Shall I just forget my phobia & go to Nicaragua? Everything seems to depend on Danny's having her baby, which is already displaying signs of un-born Hero stubbornness by being already 4 days late.

That word "Mother" that word "Mother" that word "Mother"!

I took Lise & Madeline to lunch together at Brennan's today & they were both fascinated by each other. It was rather a contest between the three of us to try & get in a word -- not just gossip & clothes, either! We rather pride ourselves (that word "Mother"!) Ann just came for the nth time up to me to get herself un-buttoned "Mother" & I raised my left hand rather abruptly to do so while still writing & she jumped 10', expecting a blow, I expect.

Your father says he has just found the yacht he wants. Dream on, McNutt -- a Nevins 40' yawl. Gads! Listen to him rave.

We ate on the dining-room table tonight for the first time. Your father is delighted it is the right height! At last. Now all I have to do is remove that eye-sore of a mantel, mirror, "The Thinker" bronze clock & matching candelabra & that cow's-udder chandelier & we'll be pure, pure, pure. Corinne told me of a woman who sells furniture from her house & said she might be able to get rid of my old one for me. I called her this morning, & in 5 minutes she tried to sell me a complete Eng. dining-room set, complete with 12 chairs, an early Am. side-board, a gold leaf pier mirror & a Baccarat chandelier.

Love, Ma

Letter 33

Postmark 23 Apr 57

Danny had another boy at 2 AM

Dear Hel

Everyone was so glad to hear your voice yesterday. I rather forced Lou to have a party when she had not planned one. She called Sat. to say she was not, and rather hinted she wanted me to bring the gals by on Sat. to get their stuff, & when I said we would come see her Sun. afternoon, she got all confused, & hid some eggs, anyway. M.L. & Warren & Peter were not there. I couldn't go Sat. as Cyn, jr had called to say she was bringing over a record for me to hear.

Mimi, the Burrus gal and Susan Miller have all been accepted by Duke. Your poor pops is going to have to plunk down $45 to reserve her place as she will not hear from Smith until May 15, and Duke has to know by May 6th. Rackets!

Liz & Gordon and Butzie went out to dinner at Arnaud's with us the other night. We had ordered a bottle of Bordeaux, when the waiter appears with a bucket & two bottles of Mumm's Champagne -- gifts from a friend of

Mimi Hero, Mary Sue Ogg, Susan Miller

Gordon's ("Dad's Oatmeal Cookies!") who had espied him and sent it over to our table. We ended the night on the patio of the Pontchartrain with stingers, and got home at 2. Consequently, I was worthless yesterday.

Pearl telephoned the Easter Bunny disease had her (I say that, not she) so I tore thru the house like a dervish and really got it cleaned up for a change, pitching most of the chocolate eggs down the disposal to save Crin a tummy ache. Ike has given her so many new dresses her portion of my wardrobe no longer contained them, so I had the movers bring down that French Provincial wardrobe from the attic & moved the chest-of-drawers to the attic. Celeste is delighted, because now she can call her room her very own without Ann butting in to get her dresses. I will have to get out the Electrosol and go to work on the mottled varnish finish and get it down to the mahogany. All in good time. Another project!

Spring

> The old cedar in the corner of
> My garden is fooling herself.
> The vine that entwines her trunk
> And climbs to the top-post branch
> Has crowned her with a wreath
> Of yellow flowers.
> She feels young.
> And when the wind bends her down
> She looks into the pool below
> And thinks she is fruitful again

Love, Ma

Letter 34

Postmark 26 April 57

Dashing off to mail your dress, which I put a hem in, directly to Barbara air-mail. Pearl sick all week. Expecting 2 Debating Society members to spend night tonight. Mimi having large slumber party tomorrow. Life rather hectic.

Love, Ma

Letter 35

Postmark 29 Apr 57

Dear Hel

When Pops makes up his mind, things move fast. Came home yesterday & said "We leave Thursday for Merida". It is not Honduras, but the Yucatan, and we shall scramble over Mexican Mayan ruins & temples for a week. Part of the week will be spent on an island where there is a new, lush hotel with swimming pool, which I shall <u>use</u>! Don't faint. Since I have lost 15# I say to hell with the fat legs! I have been collecting a few things in case of a trip. One was a dress & coat in Vogue -- the dress a grey denim sheath with a short-sleeved straight cut coat of narrow blue, green & yellow stripes -- a dark blue short sleeved knitted sheath (wool). Boy -- it's fun being thin for the first time in my life.

Mimi had quite a blow here last night. I treated them to the candle-light routine. They arrived here after the dance around 1 A.M. About 3 A.M. the place was throbbing. I had to struggle on a dress & shoes & lipstick & run down to try & shush them up. At 5 the birds contributed to the noise, so I got up & in the kitchen were 4 gals having orange-juice & coffee. I felt shot, but love that time of day & stayed up a while talking. Finally got to sleep at 6 & was up at 10 to fix breakfast for the 10 who had spent the night. Your father predicts no good will come of the boys for during the night they played "Boheme" & the Gregorian Chant & he shook his head sorrowfully over the decadence of the present generation.

We had gone to dinner at the Miles' beforehand with Molly & Barney. Had a delicious meal of cold rare roast beef -- delicious hot oysters in a chafing dish, green salad, cheeses & vin rosé.

Ann burst into tears when she found out we were leaving Thursday as it is May Day. So we leave Friday instead. It's only a 2 hr. plane trip. I am jumping with excitement. I hope Pearl shows up tomorrow. She was gone all last week. I haven't informed her yet that she is to stay here for a week.

Ann spent the week-end at Covington with the Schanzers, so I think she is over her phobia. Seems to have had a pretty good time, but doesn't say much.

Words of wisdom for <u>all</u> mothers -- from Whitman's "Leaves of Grass"

> "He that by me spreads a wider breast than my own proves the width of my own,
> He most honors my style who learns under it to destroy the teacher"

Love,
Ma

Letter 36

Postmark 15 May 57

I will send things from N.O. to thank for the various hospitalities. Don't worry about it.

pm 15 May 57

Dear Hel

The trip was so much fun that I scarcely know where to begin. I loved the flight, & before we had scarcely settled we were in Merida & driven to the travel-agent's cool Spanish court yard & given huge glasses of fresh orange-juice. Our traveling companions to Chichen Itza (sp?) were also waiting, a young gal whom I later nicknamed "Miss Brisk" -- from California & in the ad business and an older woman "Mrs Spiritualist" from Chicago. Miss Brisk soon had us organized on a first-name basis, & we drove out to Chichen & a lovely hotel in the middle of ruins. There we got a cute little thatched-roofed cottage with a bed-room & bath & front porch. They are built of such heavy concrete walls & have tile floors & thick wooden shutters that even in the HEAT of the day they were divinely cool. The food was quite good & I threw caution away & ate everything. For two days we toured the ruins, walking up the thousands of steps the Mayans think took them closer to heaven. Another gal attached herself to us, a young one from St. Louis who had studied archeology & was quite interesting, but scared stiff of bug-life. Mrs. Spiritualist was rather a bore & pathetic, but when I found out she was 72 & looked 50 & kept up with the party where I was always dropping out, I could not help but have respect for her. Seems she has fallen in love with Jefferson Davis, so I couldn't resist telling her that my great-great something aunt, Sarah Knox Taylor, was his first wife. She looked at me in complete awe & said "oh, may I <u>touch</u>, you" which she did, while I said "oh please shake my hand. I had nothing to do with it". So she thought me <u>wonderful</u>. <u>Characters</u>!

We left there the 3rd afternoon & went on to Merida & to Ushmal. On the way to Merida, the rickety car broke a fan belt, which Alvin helped fix, it broke again, again fix, then suddenly out of water, on this hot deserted road 10 miles from Merida. Alvin & the driver plunged into the woods, & while they were gone the 2 gals & I stopped a car of Mayans & told them "aqua" -- much talk, much shaking of heads, much sympathy -- no water. Then luckily a bus -- loaded with the usual Indians, crying babies & chickens passed -- by this time the driver & your father were back from their fruitless search. The bus had cans of water. We got to Merida, got orange-juice, got another car & arrived at Ushmal around 4:30. The hotel there was also wonderful, built around a large court with a beautiful swimming pool, which I immediately got into. I was all by the "Y" & all of a sudden I looked up & every Mayan Indian working on the place was standing on the porch watching me. Then your father & the young Frenchman came in. I had seen him at Chichen but never met him so I started talking -- telling him I HATED people who lived in Paris, etc etc. So we invited him to have a drink with us before dinner. Everyone got together & we had a large party with the Frenchman treating us to wine. I told him I was an <u>expert</u> & told him the funny story about Romanée Conti, & the first thing I know he was asking me whether to buy the sweet white French or the red Spanish wine! He was a lot of fun, & so homesick. Seems he is a banker & does a lot of traveling in Central America. When he left he gave us his card with his address & telephone number in Paris to look him up when we are next there.

We toured the ruins the next morning, & these were very different from the ones at Chichen -- larger & heavier with elaborate carvings, instead of the rather shallow scratchy ones. We left after lunch, went back to Merida & spent the night, & the next morning caught the rickety local Mexican plane filled with everything <u>except</u> chickens, & went to Cozumel -- an island off the coast of Yucatan. We were met at the airport by the most extraordinary young blond man I have ever seen, & in a rush of words we found out he was an archeologist, skin-diver, movie maker & worked at the hotel to make his bed & board -- also by a retired colonel in the army. When we got to the hotel, I found it was completely deserted with the exception of the Colonel & us, and then started the 3 days that were the most fun. Every night the 4 of us had drinks & ate in the court yard, & the more I knew Bob & the Colonel the better I liked them. We got to know each other immediately, & I feel as if I have known them all my life. Look for Bob Marx on television -- adventures in skin diving, or finding buried treasures on sunken ships.

Marie Louise & Cynthia have seen some. He is so genuine, so naïf, so brilliant that everything we did with him was fun. Of course, he gets skewered right & left & doesn't understand why. Nothing matters to him except unearthing buried treasures & "Wonders"—dangling one from each finger. He keeps wondering how to "bury" them. He was crushed when your father caught only 2 fish on the fishing trip---each about 20# however. He had flown in from the jungle a black baby monkey who arrived sick & terrified & I was speaking severely to him as to the proper way to raise his "baby". He was also expecting a parrot in the next few days, & someone had sent him a pirate's hat & he has plans of strolling the streets of Cozumel with the hat on head & parrot on shoulder. I have promised to send him some gold hoop earrings. What a child!

The Colonel was charming & full of fascinating tales as he had lived all over the world. Have decided that living surrounded by men is the life for me! When we left Sat morning I was close to tears. Loved them both.

Got home to find everything in good condition, except for the fact that Crin was white & sick because Scrabble had disappeared. I had to rock her for 2 days, & she

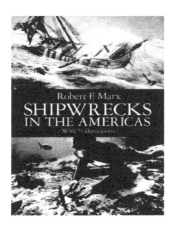

doesn't let up yet. It tears me to pieces. We have put an ad in the papers but I am afraid it is futile. I shall have to get another for her.

Your mother is now <u>important</u>. Mrs Philip Werlein phoned today to tell me I had been elected to a 3 yr. term to the board of the Philharmonic Symphony Society. I screeched "Why <u>Me</u>" & almost dropped in a faint. Gads! Janet Yancy, Mrs. Lawrence Williams, Mrs. Edgar Stern etc. etc., move over.

Love, Ma

NEW CHAIRMAN of the N. O. Symphony Women's Committee is Mrs. Alvin Hero, right, who was photographed with, from top to bottom, Mesdames William Eddins, recording secretary; G. Arthur Seaver, new board member, and Monroe Lyons, the committee's retiring chairman.

The New Chair

She's President, He'll Be Hero

BY LAURRAINE GOREAU
Item Women's Editor

Just dipping into a subject can be a deplorable thing, feels Mrs. Alvin A. Hero, president-designate of the Women's Committee of the New Orleans Philharmonic Symphony.

"I'm thinking of the marmalade case in our family," she explained. "Awful w h i l e it lasted."

"One of my daughters read somewhere that there was a remarkable amount of Vitamin P in orange rind.

"Immediately she began consuming quantities of what up to then had been safely my private stock, an imported brand that was quite expensive.

"Ate it by the jarful. But fortunately it didn't last."

* * *

THE VIGOROUS Mrs. Hero has no intention of "just dipping" into her new post, even though it creates its own brand of family crisis.

"My husband says he's prepared to take over in any emergency. But with five girls . . . that adds up to a lot of emergencies."

"I may lose a husband," she added t h o u g h t f u l l y, but brightened when an old hand at symphony work, Marilyn Barnett, assured her that various chairmen had been voicing that fear for years, but

MRS. ALVIN A. HERO

none had actually lost a husband yet.

The time-consuming post becomes Mrs. Hero's on June 4. She s u c c e e d s Mrs. Monroe Lyons, who steered the widely varied women's projects for five years.

* * *

MRS. HERO hopes her child-rearing theory will stand the test of the s t r e n u o u s year ahead.

"It's a sort of two-phase idea," she explained.

"Up to the age of 10-12, I believe in really stern discipline, to form the right basic ideas.

"After that, it's 'trust and a latch key.'

* * *

"THERE'S NO curfew, but if one is to be late, a telephone call is in order.

By "s t e r n discipline," she doesn't mean a hairbrush, she added.

"By the t i m e my fifth daughter came, I'd learned the value of a dirty look.

"I recommend it as much more effective than a spanking, especially from mother."

* * *

VEERING to Symphony topics, the president-to-be said she was "very excited" about the new Junior Committee of younger women.

"They have lots of interesting ideas and lots of energy."

She expects to continue the major Women's Committee projects, including the youth concerts, free Delgado concerts, cook's tour of kitchens, lecture previews, book fair, etc.

"But we'll have some new special events, too," she promised.

* * *

NOT WAITING for her official start, Mrs. Hero has already begun lining up various chairmen, mulling projects and problems, and generally reviving up her considerable energies for high gear by June 4, her take-over date.

She doesn't expect to see too much of her family for awhile, but she hopes that situation's squared away.

That helpful husband, you know, . . . "He's never been a mother—but he's ready to try now."

New Orleans Symphony's Committee of 100 To Promote Subscriptions

Letter 37

Postmark 17 May 57

Friday

Dear Hel

The first week of home-life after a vacation, no matter how short, is always grim, & this has proven no exception. Crin has been so white & sick over Scrabble, the telephone has been ringing all day with old lady anti-vivisectionist cranks who talk for hours about "cat-traps" & weep over the phone, and I suddenly find myself having to go way out Gentilly way to pick up a passel of cats for an old woman who has no way to bring them to the cat-lady on Jackson Ave. With no companion Crin has been under foot with questions all day, & your father wonders why I start having screaming fits at 6 P.M.

Crin with Squealer

Well, I finally got her another kitten from a woman on Marengo St. & we picked it out & had it in the car before she told us its name was "Squealer"! However, Crin is happy again, altho not eating a thing except chocolate milk 2 or 3 times a day, & I have to rock her at night again.

Mimi and I are at swords' point. She can't make up her mind about a party, wants something "unusual". It ends up with her saying at night "Oh I don't want one" and me saying "Good!" and then the whole thing starting over again at breakfast. I suggested a lunch at Brennan's with the 18 gals, & that was fine at 8 AM -- at 10 PM someone else was having a lunch -- someone suggested a watermelon party, which does not appeal in the least to me -- all those rinds that won't burn! A watermelon party is no good unless you have a pool to jump into after you get over the fights -- or that was the case in the "olden days".

We see by your checks that you have paid an initiation fee to KD. What a subtle way to tell us.

Mimi plunked down her invitations for me to do, I sit down this morning <u>expecting</u> a list with <u>addresses</u>, and what? <u>Nothing</u>. Not even a name. You have me spoiled.

     Love,
      Ma

Letter 38

Postmark 27 October 1958
Sunday

Dear Gals:

A few triumphs to make the job worthwhile come up every now and then. I put on a party for the press last Tuesday, having gotten a donation of absinthe, butler etc. for free. Did I write this to you before? It suddenly sounded familiar. It was at the Harold Levy's apartment in the French Quarter, and the bar was set up in the courtyard, and the food, which I catered, in the dining-room. And I think I impressed them with the smoked turkey, cheese fondue, hot shrimp, and red-fish vinaigrette. The table did look festive with the two dishes with alcohol burners under them etc., etc. However, HARDLY ANY PRESS SHOWED UP! Some of my dear "friends" were making nasty cracks about "Stella Dallas" parties, etc., but the few who did show could not but be impressed by the amount of trouble we had gone to for them. And a Mr. Kennedy, who had earlier gotten me to pin an honor in his lapel from a French Chef, (he belongs to the Taste-Vin society) when he left, raved about the food. The piece-de resistance, however, was a blurb in the music critic, Sim Meyer's, column two days later – Quote –At the cocktail party at the Harold Levy's the other night, given by the W.C.N.O. Ph. Sy. S. for members of the press, T.V. and radio, no one exuded more charm and personality than the new chairman of the women's committee, the <u>bubbly</u> Mrs. Hero. Unquote.

Marilyn Barnett sent me a note saying he had called her the next day and said I was attractive, sharp, witty, and the only woman he had met in N.O. in two years who interested him in the least. Don't get worried – he's not the marrying kind! However, all of this may mean some good publicity for us, which we need. It has not, tho, made me very popular with the rest of the women, who were teasing me like mad at a meeting the other day. Ah, well, I have something to show the grandchildren!

The grim, hard work goes on every day, with no let up that I can see, and people constantly calling and telling me about the mistakes I have made, in the sweetest tone of voice, and I thank them for pointing them out to me in the sweetest tone of voice right back. The Benny Benefit is not doing at all well; we are only up to $12,000, and with $6,000 expenses that does not mean a thing. The women are supposed to get the first $10,000, $8,500 of which they turn back as their orchestra commitment for the coming year. I have been able to sell only 10 tickets, and gotten a $25 donation, which is peanuts, and I get nasty cracks from my chairman. We were in Neville Levy's office the other day and the men put him to work on the telephone, and he raised $600 in 15 minutes. But he said it cost him, personally, $400 to give the time. I was fascinated listening to how power gets things done, and simply sat there giggling. I would hate to have the first drive that I headed be a failure, but with tickets at $25, $20, $15, $10, and $5, it is a difficult job, not to mention $100 for

Hélène Working on the Benny Benefit October 19, 1958

box-seats! (Your father and I have 2, Poor man, he can't really afford to keep me in this!) The first concert is Tuesday; we have to go first to a Curtain Time party at the Pont[chartrain]. And then a welcome reception after the concert, so it means a long, trying night, especially now that I have to be BUBBLY every time I show myself in public!

I am afraid that I got too flip with Mr. Hilsberg the other night when he came up to tell me good-by at the party. I said to him "I may not be much as a worker, Mr. Hilsberg, because I am really all for fun. Let's have FUN, this year, Mr. Hilsberg". And he gave me a look out of his little Slavic eyes that made me want to run away, then he bent over and kissed my hand and said "I know, we will, Mrs. Hero". Truth is, I am working, I think, hard, and Janet Yancey told me I was really the most conscientious chairman they had ever had. Or am I repeating the few compliments that occasionally get tossed my way?

All of this, is, of course, hard on the family, for whom I have little energy left over. Your father is gorgeous! It's hard on him when I collapse after dinner, but he has taken over the two youngsters, and yesterday when I forgot all about a birthday-party that Crin was to go to (she did get there) Crin went to him when he came back from fishing and said "Mother forgot; I wish you had been here because I know you would not have forgotten", and I wanted to cry. Ann is getting after me about Crin going to school with no buttons on her clothes; maybe I will learn how to do both before the year is up. I did buy Ann a nice-looking red coat and hat, and Crin a cute dark-blue Breton sailor that she wears well back and with an elastic under her chin, and went to church today in a cute Eaton suit that Ike bought and she looked so smart. I have had to hide most of the clothes that Ike got her this year. I should take them back. The one he got in Lancaster is the worst; huge red roses all over. She, of course, had to wear it the first day, but I have it in a box with the others. With those around, she refuses to wear the simple ones I have gotten, and Ann says I simply have to do something, so I have. Hel, your father says you may go to New York on Thanksgiving. Congratulations on the marvelous mark in Psychology. I am sure you will catch on to the new teaching methods. Your father is saying yan, yan, yan to me, and I told you that R.M was a better college!

       Love,
              Ma.

Letter 39

Postmark 10 Nov 58

Dear Gals:

The past week has been one of great excitement. I got on my uppers due to the apathy displayed by the members of the Board on the Jack Benny Benefit and called an emergency meeting at my house on Monday to see if they could not be made to at least sell a few tickets, or at most buy some themselves. Well, Helene Godchaux gets up and proposes that we send a recommendation to the big board that we cancel the whole thing. I wanted to throw up and could scarcely get out with Is the motion seconded, which it was, and then someone suggested before we took a vote the matter be further discussed, when in walks my friend Eileen Wilson, waving her arms and saying, "I have $1000 for the Benefit", which changed the entire picture. It was as exciting as a Western, with the hero arriving at the last minute to save the heroine. Well, that motion was defeated unanimously, after that. Then another motion was made, demanding a meeting with the Executive Board of the Big Board to discuss the Benefit, and a telegram was sent to all the members. The meeting broke up, and I was weak. Eileen and Marilyn and I went to the Pontchartrain and dived into martinis and giggled about how we were making the Women's Committee sit up and take notice, also the Big Board. This demanding of a meeting has never been done in the history of the organization. Then Marilyn calls the office, and it seems Mrs. Ladreyt is having a fit because the answers to the telegrams were pouring in to the office and she could not find me. She had to find a place for the meeting, which was to be in two days, and I was to call the women and she the men and women of the B.B. The other two almost corrupt me, and I go downtown with them to see Gigi, when I decide on Canal Street that I have to be home in case Ladreyt calls, so I dash off and get into a taxi while they gape at me. I get home at 3:30, check in with Ladreyt, who still has not been able to get confirmation of the Board Room at N.B.C. Bank, find Mr. Morris has been calling me, call him back and get a "Let's not get hysterical, Mrs. Hero" to which I answer "ARE we hysterical, Mr. Morris" to which he answers about the motion made to cancel, to which I answer, yes, but that motion was defeated unanimously.

Well the next day Rita Odenheimer and I got to Roger Wilson's office, meet Eileen there, and the upshot of that day is that she raises ANOTHER $1000! She gave Rita and me names of men to tramp around to, while she tramped and called, and all I could get was $90 and Rita $190, so she did all the rest! Her husband is a very rich oil executive, and all the money was gotten from his friends, who had never contributed to the Symphony before. It was the most exciting day I ever spent in my life. So at the meeting of the two boards the next day, we had made Neville Levy so ashamed of himself that he came in with $350 more pledged; the first money he had turned in in a week! And Mr. Morris got a standing ovation for THE WOMEN from the Big Board, and then when the meeting was over they all came to Eileen and shook her hand and said "If we only had more workers like you!" I was shaking with happiness. This is the gal whom I was warned against, and whom I have never heard a kind word said of, and whom I put on my executive board without consulting a soul.

After the Board meeting, the gals on the steering committee, Neville Levy and I go back to Roger Wilson's office, go over some other names, and repair to lunch at Antoine's before starting out. The gals to do the procuring are the cream of the crop young and attractive, and I never felt so like a Madam as I walked into Antoine's with them, all heads turning to look, and me stalking behind as if I were cracking a whip. The upshot of that afternoon of work was $250 more. I hate, really, this business of going into men's offices. It is very difficult to get past the stony eyes of the receptionists without stating your business, and if you state your business you are sunk. Some flatly refuse to see you if you do not. Well, I am going again on Tues and Wed with them across the river to [get] some more names that Roger has given his little wifie.

The opening concert was a tremendous success, and so was the party afterwards. The subscriptions are higher this year than ever in history, and the air was filled with a kind of electricity. Have I written you all this? I forget. I think I did. So I will tell you about the scrumptious dinner-party I had Thursday with some Symphony friends, and Martha and Poche. I had duck and wild rice and mushrooms and salad and Cordon wine and a gorgeous mousse that I made, and which was much admired by the Commande of the Taste-Vin who was here. It was just one of those days when everything turned out; I am really due a few. And Martha Miles pulled me into the pantry and said it was truly a BEAUTIFUL party, and how much she liked my new friends; what interesting people they were; and your father did not object too much to sitting in the drawing-room with the candle-light treatment, or eating by candle-light only, as he did not have to carve, and everyone had a FIT over a duck apiece and your father did not mind my using brandy snifters, and even came across with an extra special Courvoisier for the occasion. And we all had FUN and it lasted until 1:30, in spite of the fact that it was a Thursday.

Well, next week Cliburn comes. And the week after, the Benny Benefit, with a party at the Stern's the day before and a supper after the concert after the Benefit, to which I shall wear my gorgeous new orange chiffon. So after all the suffering, a bit of fun.

Love,
Ma

You got invited to two debut parties, which I refused; one by the Freemans and one by the Logans & Tomskeys which I refused for you.

> Mrs. Alvin Hero selected an apricot color chiffon gown made with an Empire line where it was caught in folds. With the dress she wore a matching scarf. Mrs. Benjamin Frank-

Letter 40

Postmark 1 Dec 58

Dear Gals:

Well, I have had a week, practically, anyway since last Tues. free from Symphony and I have spent it in the bottom of high-ball glasses. I had another Board meeting Tues., and it was a record one; got the gals rushed thru in 1/2 hour, and every one congratulated me. It was a meeting full of joy and pleasure, with good news all around; $5,000 over subscriptions, $4000 over Symp. for Children, and we made our orchestra commitment of $8,500 out of the Benny-fit (Mims, I loved your card). Now I have to set a fire under Wilson and get the Fair Grounds benefit under way. My Maintenance gal is in Cal. so I have to do some ground work for her until she gets back, and Marc Anthony came up with an attractive offer for us that I shall have to get approved and then find a chairman for if it is. Well, that's all a lot better than hanging around the house reciting a litany of my faults to myself all day long, which is what I do when I am not doing anything.

M.L. had a scrumptious dinner on Thanksgiving, and I started out so pure with just the vermouth part of a martini, and the Tavel Rose, and after lunch I succumbed to the Moocow (pronounced, not spelled) Brandy that Lou brings every year to Warren as a special treat, so was dancing & talking too much. Leeds and his party came screaming down the street and joined us and I find I am famous; a dirty word is known as an "Helene" and they use my name instead of being blasphemous; seem, this has been going on since 2 yrs. ago cause Leeds said Molly was giving me extravagant compliments about myself to my face and that I stood it as long as I could and said "oh s--t, Molly" Ah, me FAME!

We went to the Zemurray gal's wedding. It was rather small and quiet and I did not see until the next day that Alta was in the wedding-party. I ducked the bridesmaids all except for Lyn Hayward, who was at the end. Lyn gave me her bouquet of gardenias, which is still slowly getting yellow in the living-room. Can't bear to throw it out.

The Rayburn Monroes' reception was a good, family kind of party, with a band and nice feeling of having the whole thing done at home instead of at a public place. We did not stay long, as there are only a very, very few of THAT GROUP whom I talk to, or talk to me. Something funny happened; I had on a hat I had sent off for last summer in the N.Y. Times for $6.95 to pep up the $10 chartreuse wool I had gotten on sale last year; it has greenish grapes, leaves and white flowers on a band and it looks expensive. Hunter Leake said "Why, Helene, you look like Lady Bacchus", and he gave it a broad A, and I said, who is that some old english aristocrat? And Geo. Williams admired it and then floored me by saying, it is something like the dark blue one you had last year! So I told him he was a man with a soul if he could remember a lady's hat for 1 year, and if he didn't mind I'd fall in love with him. And Mrs. Lemann said here comes the gal who is known for her unusual outfits! and two people said they always like to see me because I was their PET, and a young man complimented me on my speedy wit, so I should not feel depressed today, but do,

Love in a hurry to get Ann at a party,

Ma

Lady Bacchus

Letter 41

Postmark 12 Jan 59

Dear Gals:

Glad to get your letters about safe arrival. I am, of course, bogged down with THE WORK, as we are now in maintenance fund drive period. Had two lunches last week, one with the women at Nela Battley's, which was beautifully done with delicious food, and another at the St. Charles, where I SAT AT the speaker's table and was introduced by Bill Ricciutti as THAT DYNAMIC, INTELLIGENT LEADER OF THE WOMEN, OUR HELENE! Nothing like having a good friend at the head of the drive. Then had lunch with the Wilson gal and Marilyn Barnett at the Fountain Lounge, where M. talked turkey about the Race Track Benefit, and she has agreed to do it, on her own terms, which means I have a lot of work ahead of me recruiting the women to work on it, which she, as chairman, should do. Oh well, as Helene Godchaux said of me, she does everyone's dirty work! Seems I am getting a reputation. Went to pick up Crin at Cindy Samuel's today and Mr. Samuel said he heard me given the supreme compliment the other day; says they were talking about getting a Membership Chairman (he did not say to what, but must have something to do with the Navy) and three people in unison and simultaneously said my name, but he said someone said I had already turned them down. Can't imagine what it is all about, but was glad for the compliment. Still have the shakes about this job. Sat next to Mr. Edgar Stern at the Kick Off lunch and bowled him over by remembering Edgar Jr's nurse, English, Miss Shields, and he spent the whole lunch giving me her life history and how she ended up in jail.

Celeste had a slumber party last night and spent Friday making two delicious cakes, a chocolate and a coconut and cookies and a custard, and only 4 people came! Seems everyone was bogged down with two books to read and reports to make.

Have an Ex. Board meeting tomorrow where I am going to present to them the scheme for progression of officers that I read about and typed up in 10 copies this summer. It is time to choose a new chairman, and Martha says it is up to me but I want to get the system changed, and try to make this a tighter organization, and also to make the top job a bit easier for successors. Big board meeting Wed. Have to have A COFFEE here next Friday and am gnashing my teeth. Am having the Maestro and Mrs. Hilsberg and the Ricciutti's and the Hansons on Sat., am going to two lunches and after concert party next week, so the time will be filled.

Your busy, loving and negligent
Ma

Mrs. Stern learned for the first time I had 5 kids, and almost flipped and wanted to know how I was doing all this work, so I said, my children are being neglected.

Letter 42

Postmark 22 Jan 59

Dear Gals

Exhaustion again. Busy times with cutting radio tapes, Board meetings (3) lunches and dinners after concerts. I just heard myself over the radio, and my voice did sound oh quite quite cultured and I did make an effort to enunciate clearly. M. Barnett said rather like Katie Hepburn. However, the guy threw an unrehearsed question at me in the end and complete confusion on top of fear made the answer, how long will the maintenance fund last, fly out of my head and there is this embarrassing pause where, had it been on television you would have seen me flinging my hands around and mouthing when, when,

when, to the guy doing the interviewing. He finally caught on and got me out of it by saying something fast. Whew!

Monday I started out at 11 to the Camellia lunch and quartet, where I again sat at the speakers table and was very longly and humiliatingly introduced by Mrs. Cutting, who delved into the courage it took to take over after 6 yrs. of Martha, how Mrs. Hero had done an immense amount of studying (how did she know), how humorous my board meetings were (the humor has left; I am very, very business-like) and ended up by saying Our Heroine. Gads. Then an Ex. Board Meeting of the big board where I had to introduce 4 things for their approval, then a Board Meeting, which lasted until 5. They asked me to do it again for another year, and I accepted. The next day, there was a rehearsal and then an after rehearsal lunch given by the Jr. Committee. It was really a success, with good food and well set up. The only thing I found wrong was the fact that all the young gals herded themselves into one corner and made no effort to talk to and meet the musicians, so I thought I would set a good example by going up to a bunch of them and saying it was turning into a typical N.O. party with all the men on one side and all the women on the other and as far as I was concerned I thought each gal should grab a guy, and so I grabbed one and took him over and said It's easy, all you do is go up and grab, and then I sat at a table with all the men. But no one else did it, and I shall make a very strong point of that at the next meeting. My friend Mr. Cicirelli, who did the drawing, sat opposite me and said So this is the auxiliary to the auxiliary, eh. So

I said, yes, so he said, well I won't say anything, so I said, you don't have to, I can read your mind. The one I grabbed turned out to be a very attractive tuba player from N.Y. and we yacked and yacked and I learned quite a good deal from him. I had the best time at the party, and he was the last musician to leave. My new hat-bar shiny sailor had made a hit. Funny, men are always complimenting me on my hats. I guess they notice them because no one else wears one. After the concert we went to the Manheim's for a party, and it was too sticky sticky. Again, I had a good time because Mr. Cillini sp? who conducts the opera sat at my table with Alvin and another guy (one table had two women only at it so I did all right) and he is vastly amusing and loads of fun, a far cry from our own Mr. Hilsberg. Think I'll switch to opera!

The supper was excellent, with wine, and everything was beautifully served, and the only hitch was when Mr. Manheim started everyone off by getting me to go into the dining room with the young pianist Johannsen who was the guest of honor, and no food had been put on the table. Mrs. Manheim carried it off very calmly by saying my husband refuses to be embarrassed by anything, so we stood around while the food was brought on. This morning I tore out after breakfast to go wish the orchestra bon voyage at the bus station as they left for the 3 weeks eastern tour. And in bed at home all day.

We had a dinner party last Saturday with the Hilsbergs, Ricciuttis and Hansons (he's the dean of the music school at Newcomb and she plays the violin in the orchestra) and everyone had a good time except me, because I threw two new and hard things at Pearl to make, Marchand du vin sauce and hollandaise, and Ann had a spend the night and Celeste had a spend the night and they piled into the kitchen and Pearl did not put the roast on until <u>after</u> the guests came, and it was hours of drinking, and they do not drink much, and I left everything up to Wesley and he just put cold slabs of roast on an un-parsleyed platter instead of bringing in the whole roast, and it took a long time to pass it briskly around the wrong side of the table and everything more or less cold it being the coldest night of the year with the wind whistling through all the big windows. However, I made my biscuit tortoni which always makes a hit and Mrs. Hilsberg exclaimed and exclaimed over it and everyone took twice, and everyone stayed until one so I guess the disasters of the meal were overlooked. Pearl's sauces were very, very good. Doris Hanson wrote me a note and said it was a most stimulating and interesting party, and Mrs. Hilsberg phoned and said how much they liked the small, intimate parties, and Bill said isn't it nice when everyone clicks, so I guess all the moaning I did over the food went unnoticed. I cannot have class unless I do it every day, so hereafter, back to the side-board service.

Hel, you may have the gals, but the house is a mess and I don't have time to do anything about it, and only if you are to be here the whole time because I cannot do anything about them and you don't want a party because I still have not recovered from Xmas, and I am having to have 50 women over here for a coffee Friday, the new Telephone Committee. Gads.

Your CHAIRMAN FOR TWO YEARS MA.

WOMEN NEAR GOAL OF $25,000

Raise $20,000 in Symphony Fund Drive

The Women's Division of the New Orleans Philharmonic-Symphony current campaign, under the leadership of Miss Cornelia Wattley, has reached 80 per cent of its quota.

As announced by general chairman, I. William Ricciuti, the women have raised $20,000. Their goal is $25,000.

"These women, with 22 chairmen and a total of 216 workers are to be commended and have done a splendid job," Ricciuti said.

"I am distressed," Ricciuti addedd "that the men in this campaign for the orchestra's maintenance fund have not done as well."

—Photo by C. F. Weber.

THE GOOD NEWS on the campaign waged by her division of the New Orleans Philharmonic-Symphony fund drive is given I. William Ricciuti, general chairman, by Mrs. Alvin Hero, chairman of the women's committee.

Letter 43

Postmark 2 Mar 59

Hel -- Congratulations on the good grades! And the new job! Wotta Gal! I am bursting the buttons

Dear Gals:

Pound out a late letter to you both -- seems I haven't written for so long. The past two weeks have had me going every day, and also preparing for the "do" that was here last Monday. The week before I got a guy to wash the face of the house and it gave your pa the screaming weemies because I got him fast and he did it fast, for $25. Then I got a crew of three gardeners who worked all day clipping and weeding the long-neglected garden, then I got Melvin and he & I waxed and shined, and then 2 pianos and 100 chairs were moved in and the two gals who were to play came for two days to practice, and brought critics and page-turners. And then came the day of the function -- beautiful in the morning -- warm -- so I opened up all the windows to let the outside in; so guess what -- yep -- a squall let loose and blew thru the house as the people began pouring in -- literally! As the rain came, so did ladies, ladies, ladies! At conservative count, I must have had 150 here. They were in the hall, dining-room and small living room. Isaac Stern was to come to lecture -- his plane was late. There was a long delay. The food and sherry ran out -- I sent Celeste to the store for a gallon of "Gallo's" while one of the entertainment ladies ran out for more cakes. We set up an emergency coffee-pouring stand on the back porch -- which I had opened up and decorated with rented yellow chrysanthemums and table and cloth to put cakes on and stuff. Mrs. Holbrook and I were having running nasty fights all along -- gads! she brought paper napkins with roses and forget-me-nots on them! Mary said she said "Humph! I have been coming to Mrs. Hero's for one year now, but I never saw that coffee service before. Does it belong to her?"

The Slow Pouring Coffee Pot

I had borrowed Ike's. Then she said to me "That coffee pot of yours pours very slowly." No answer from me. "Well, I guess the women can wait". No answer from me. I began drinking the sherry in the kitchen and poking my tongue at her behind her back. Marilyn was having hysterics. When she left the room I began a long tirade against her, and in the middle of -- and Mrs. Holbrook said, who should walk in, so I quickly said and Mrs. Holbrook, will we have enough Oh, Mrs. Holbrook I am so worried. The sherry made me silly, and I started telling Marilyn about a strip-tease I did here one night, forgetting the good Baptist ladies present, and God-damning all over the place. Isaac Stern arrived, talked, and left, and I never even saw him. Mrs. Holbrook and her sister were making so much noise in the kitchen about putting out the cakes that some one had to come and shut them up. I stood and drank sherry. I took one look at the crowds in the dining-room and did not emerge until almost everyone had left. I was late with the "presentation" bouquets for the two piano gals and rushed them up after they had left the drawing-room. Then I hear from everyone the next day that it was THE BEST program ever given by the Women's Committee -- and I get a thank-you note saying how charming and gracious I am, and how I so quickly arise to emergencies and am not fazed in the least by too many people, rain, and a late guest-artist!! And in the same week meetings, Maintenance Fund drive, Renewals to set up, lunches to go to to listen to new schemes for making money, and Ann telling me, "Mother, one day you are going to find us in the gutter". Bill Ricciutti said for the Very first time, the Maintenance is making its goal -- both men's and women's!!!!!!

Love, Ma

Letter 44

Postmark 13 Mar 59

ME POOR NEGLECTED GALS!

I have just simply been stretched out in bed ever since that ladies' "Do". And knowing that I had to start in organizing for next year. Didn't have energy to go swimming. Got the lovely news that we would have to produce $12,500 next year. Have been screaming "Taxation without representation" to the men on the Ex Board. Had my own board meeting, which resulted in a meeting with the men to explain the budget. Went to Ex. Meeting and made a mathematical analysis on the spot that resulted in dead silence. Got them to agree that a representative of the Women's Comm. should be on the Budget Comm. Hives.

Well, had a dinner party here Sat. and it was the best food that Pearl produced. Went sailing that afternoon instead of hanging around the kitchen and being nervous and making Pearl nervous, so have decided to do it that way hereonout. Been so good lately that I hit the Brandy and pulled out all the stops and gave imitations of Hilsberg and neverneverneverstoppedtalking. The two gals who were here were kind enough to phone a couple of days later after they had recovered to say they had had fun. The kindness of people sometimes overwhelms me. Well, it's funny. I am saying the same things I have been saying for years and years, and now I get told all the time that I am well informed, intelligent, can talk on ohsomanysubjects, and was even told that if it hadn't been for me such and such a party would have been ververydull. At last! I am going out with intelligent people.

A Jr. group to the Jr. group has been made. Namely, Celeste's class which has come forth to do some placard showing on the stage of the auditorium for the kick-off of the renewals drive on Tues. I find that the Jr. group (mostly Jr Leaguers too) say (only they are too refined to say it) that it makes them feel like prostitutes to parade around. They won't even stand by the ticket office without their husband's protection. Gads!

I have been working all day on this stuff, after my "vacation" (which wasn't a real rest, because the phone rings all day) and I am still in a wrapper, have not taken your father's suit to the cleaner etc.etc. Am going to a party for Serkin Tues. and will also meet Alfred Knopf who is visiting them. So have been doing a lot of reading and memorizing new words and phrases and stuff so I'll be erudite. Went to one for Mr. Howard Hanson. He and his wife were that rare combination of charm, common sense, sense of humor and non-temperament that is not usual in these artists. However, did not see much of them at the party as they were monopolized by the BIG DOGS, but was asked to take them home. Knopf is visiting the Barnetts, who are having the party. Mr. Barnett and I are in love with each other! It's so nice!

Ann is having her recital tonight, so all the family is going. Luckily, Lou gave Ann & Crin a lovely new dress and coat, pale spring green coat and pale spring green flowers on white dress and I got Crin her Easter shoes yesterday, so maybe we will all look all right.

Love, love, love
Ma

Letter 45

Postmark 21 Sep 59

Dear Gals,

Thanks for the letter, Hel. I have not been doing anything, so this letter will be dull. Maury moved in last Wed. night, and I scarcely know she is here. She is really delightful and she and Celeste seem to get on very well together. I had to give Celeste Hell because she took my car without asking and then somehow wound up at Hunter Leake's for dinner, so when she and Maury got home about 11, I blew all the stacks and the air was quite smokey for a while and I have forbidden her the use of the car for one month.

Mimi, the dress is alright. I cloroxed all the stains out myself and there is nary a one left. Hel, I cannot find the round pin. Ask Mimi where it is. Typing on the floor is unsatisfactory. Mims, I have gotten as far as collecting paper to wrap up, and now am on the hunt for some string, and when I find some, I'll send your stuff.

Will be doing a bit of Symphony work again. The gal whom I got to do the Subscriptions asked me to work, and Janet Yancey asked me to take a guest artist for dinner in Jan. A woman violinist, and she gave me quite a compliment; said she was supposed to be "difficult", so she was turning her over to me! And I'll have a Program

ELECTED chairman of the Women's Division of the New Orleans Philharmonic Symphony Society, MRS. RUDOLPH J. WEINMANN, right, previews a busy summer with the outgoing chairman, MRS. ALVIN A. HERO. Chairmen of various committees will be busy soon on subscriptions, program advertising, chamber music concerts and a revision of the by-laws.

Passing the Gavel, Spring 1959

here in March. Am looking forward to something to do. Everyone keeps jumping on me about being "thin", and makes me feel as if I am one jump from the hospital. I still haven't lost that 4 lbs! But then, I am still on the summer beer kick. Wish the weather would get cool. Went swimming at the Yacht club, and it was windy, and the water was very cool and I did enjoy it.

We found a lovely old square grand piano in good condition by an ad today, and we want to send a tuner up tomorrow to see if it is tunable, but the gal is being difficult; says no one will be there because she works. We are still negotiating, and your father will try to get up there tomorrow with one on her lunch hour. If he gives the ok we'll get it, and I'll put it between the windows in the front of the drawing room where the Buhl [Boulle] cabinet now is. I hope this one works out, because it will fit the house well.

                Love,
                      Ma

Letter 46

Postmark 28 Sept 59

Dear Gals:

You would all be proud, proud of sister Ann. She was elected class representative on the Student Council, and she is making such good grades and is so kinda organized this year that you can audibly hear the brains ticking. Big differences in Crin too. Everyone seems to have grown up this year except mother. Celeste is studying up a storm what with all those erudite courses she is taking. Me, back to the 1st to learn to spell! Maury has just slipped in and I feel as if she has been here always. She would like to stay here instead of ever going to the dorm, because she has gotten used to us, too, and she and Celeste get along very well, indeed, but she seems to think her mother won't let her. I'll cross that one when the time comes.

Went to the Moyer gal's wedding reception. It was dull, and I was just beginning to have fun with Herbert Williams who asked me if I had on my dancing pants and I went into an act and he gave one of those wild rebel yells and I said I just love his mating call, don't you, and your father said, time to go home.

Ann took me swimming at the closed C.C. pool this afternoon, and I met, Mimi, the Mrs. De laVerne you met this summer, and she said, Mimi said I was just like you. THANKS!!!!! [Mimi did not say that.] The water was delicious and I swam and swam and I think Homer Dupuy thought I was going to have a heart attack. He said, your stroke is still very good, but don't have one!

The women's comm. work keep me, thank god, busy this week, what with Finance comm. meeting Mon., Subscription drive meeting Tues. and Board meeting Wed. Marilyn and I are having lunch together after the Wed. meeting so we can say nasty things about the over-dressed women, with under-dressed brains.

Hel, the Knit Shop said do not get impatient over your sweater, it will take quite a while to do, 5-6 weeks. I was delighted to find that they do needlepoint, so took that lovely French chair cover to be finished by them.

Love, Ma

Letter 47

Postmark 6 Oct 59

Dear Gals:

Your mother survived a week that has left her bloody and I wish I could say, un-bowed, but perhaps for a change a little humility is for the good. I had three women's committee meetings, Mon. Tues. and Wed. Wed. was the first board meeting of the new chairman, a large crowd came, including all the new attractive, young and intelligent members we voted in this year. The new chairman started with an opening speech. To my cold horror I heard from her lips oh what a wonderful set-up this is this year. I just sit back and it just gets thrown at me with no effort on my part. Now, Mrs. Hero has said that she is inefficient and last year could not possibly get around to doing everything, so we have the marvelous and well-known efficiency of Mrs. Monroe Lyons, our former chairman for 5 years to thank for this perfectly marvelous set up. I got cold, hot, weepy and throw-upy all in turn, but managed to stay calm. Rosemary Eddins, the rec. sec., threw me an agonized look of pure horror, and I thought she was going to burst into tears. I had come there prepared to make a plea for Marilyn's Press Party which had been voted against this summer. She had called the afternoon before and asked my support in doing it without the Women's Comm. I thought it over, called Bill Ricciutti that night and got his approval of the idea. When my turn came, gals, the adrenalin was up. I bit off, coldly, clearly, logically with perfect diction, the best damn argument for the party that you ever heard. I never knew I was an orator, but gals, I am! It was passed, unanimously!

Well, to top that all off, at about 7:30 that night Martha Miles called if we would come for a drink. Anything to help a suffering friend; so I dragged a protesting Alvin over, knowing in advance it was he that she wanted to talk to, but just let's be generous, eh? I won't go into the details of the night because the behavior, both hers and mine, was un-civilized and I am just forgetting it as best I can. She called me dumb, simple and stupid, among other things. I am a bit more subtle, and had fun seeing her not catch mine. Well, I left my hat there, and it got returned today; she put it on the top of the roof of the automobile in the garage. Had I been the one to do that, it would have been under the automobile!!!!

Well, what with all that I spent a sleepless night, climaxed by sudden resignation letters from both Symph. Boards.

Two days later, I called Helene Godchaux to say that I did not mean my letter to sound snippy, that she hadn't done a thing and she wanted to know what on earth had happened, and I said, nothing, just me, I was a nervous wreck and just had to put the whole thing completely out of my mind. She expressed deep regret, said that my speech had been perfectly marvelous, that every single thing that I had said made sense. And then she said, please come to the meetings. I said no, the meetings upset me, so she said, then will you let us sometimes call you up for advice. I burst out laughing, and said that was the nicest thing anyone had ever said to me. And she said, no, I mean it! That from a woman who has worked 20 years for this organization and is one of the most intelligent people I know! Well, I moped around the house for two days. Finally, Sat. night, I called Helene and asked her to send back that list of prospects to me. She burst out laughing, and said you are a riot! And then I said, do you think it will be alright for me to write Mary Vic and ask her to tear up my letter of resignation, and she said yes so violently I almost dropped the receiver. So then I wrote a humble letter to Bill and asked him to let me stay on. So I have learned many, many lessons this week.

Well, I had fun, too. Fri. night had dinner with the Breits and the Tom Jordans and George Frierson and Cath. Westfeldt. Well, Mrs. J. and I tangled. What a strange combination of brilliance and social slop that woman is. At one point I found myself flinging an arm and accusing finger at her, violently and then I burst out laughing and said, here I swore before I came over tonight just to be the simple, nice little socialite and not get into any arguments. It is impossible. Anyone who asks me back has a strong stomach. And both Yawl and Va. said, we wouldn't have you any other way. And later on that night Yawl said, I am always hearing so many nice things about you, Helene, you have so many people who so genuinely like you. So I said, sometimes I think I haven't a friend in the world. I live surrounded by people who disapprove of me, who say why don't you just, can't you really be, won't you really try to -- And he said PLEASE DON'T!!!!!!!

Last night I had fun, too. Lila and Morris Newman had us to the Yacht club dinner for the Chicago and N.O. L16 race celebration, which we won. I sat next to the world's champion, and pretty soon found out just what kind of man he is and how he does his racing. And guess what, Polly, old Polly, whom I have never heard spoken of except disparagingly, that he always smelled like the monkeys he sold, I unearthed something there, too. Somehow, the subject of photography came up, and he mentioned that when he was a young man in N.Y. he did quite a bit of it. I took a long shot, and asked him if he had known Stieglitz. Well, that did it. They were close friends and rivals, so I learned one hell of a lot. At dinner, he was across the table from me, and he announced, I have been having an artistic conversation, and I haven't had one in 30 yrs!!!!! No wonder, hanging around the Y.C.! Morris had said, earlier, the people out here aren't really very stimulating, so sometimes one drinks more than one should to get through it, so I said, well, Morris, you have asked the Heroes out tonight, so he laughed and said, that helps, that does help.

And I also got called one of the best looking gals in the room by another Chicagoan, the other being Lila, who was sitting on the other side of the Champ, and the man across the table wanted to know how come he had managed to get the two best looking. So, I said, I have always said that the only Southern gentlemen are the Northern ones.

As I say, the week was WILD!!!!!!

Love,
Ma.

Letter 48

Postmark 12 Oct 59

Dear Gals:

We have started the job of fixing up the house across the river. We went over yesterday with Raymond, and Melvin met us there. It is incredible. They cut the grass away from the house, but let actual trees take over the little

The House Across the River in Belle Chasse

door yard garden I had struggled so hard to make; vines, willows, overgrown roses 10 feet high entangled in the hedge, which you couldn't see for the native stuff that had smothered it. And the bamboo is a wild nightmare; it makes an actual tunnel from the kitchen to the garage. They kept chickens on the back porch; the horse tethered to a tree near the brick retaining wall, which it kicked mostly down; an old washing-machine lies in the churned up mud that used to be grass outside the porch door. The whole house smells of chicken, cats, and dogs, and the wood-work is smeared with chicken mess. Oh, I could weep. And that couple are two college graduates! The negroes for miles are coming to take a look and just loving it. White folks without them to work for them are just as bad as they are -- you can see pure delight in their faces as they cluck sympathetic noises to me -- trash, bottles, mess. Gads! I told Alvin the next people we get we will demand references. I am going to choose wall paper for all the rooms over again, so that will be fun, and we are raising the rent to get a more desirable class.

France-Amerique had a whiz of a Wine & Cheese party at the Roosevelt Thursday. It was packed with people and tres gai. I could laugh as loud as I wanted to, because the Creole does not mind a bit of gaiety. We took the Breits whom we had gotten to join, and I was so glad their first party was a bang up one for them.

A busy week coming up. Party for Alvin, Press Party for Symp, and party that Ricciutti is having for Hilsberg.

Went swimming at Mildred's both yesterday and today. Very glad to see N.C. after all these years and find that the rumors that "N.C. is a BIG boy now" are true. He has a fine build on him. He kinda ignored me, and just ducked his little sisters around the water and did diving, but never came near me after tossing a "HI" over his shoulder to me. Allen is a love, and most friendly, and so were the two little ones. Ann & Crin came with me today, but they did not seem to have much to do with one another. Numa said he had spoken to his father in Moscow this morning.

Love,
                                                                                Ma

Letter 49

Postmark 19 Oct 59

Dear Gals:
The little house is emerging. We had gangs down there chopping bamboo, that evil, crawling, malicious plant and Raymond and Melvin tackled the rest of the front garden, pruned the crepe myrtle and chopped down volunteer trees of great girth. Some time this week I'll investigate wall paper. Am also working on this one; Ann's & Crin's room has been painted white, and I am painting those two bookcases red and will get them some bed-spreads & curtains, if I can find anything under $1,00000000.

The Press Party Wednesday had a pretty good turn out. Jack Daily looked sour, which I made bold to tell him, but no one else did. Bill Ricciutti complained about the

Absinthe so I said brother, give us the dough and we'll give you the party and who's looking whose gift horse in the mouth and he said Helene, you sure have the long needle out this year, and I said brother, I sure have, but you still like me, don't you Bill, and he threw his arms around me and said the trouble is, I LOVE you. And Scoop Kennedy said I was his favorite woman, and both the Maestro and Mrs. H. separately expressed regret that I was not doing the job again this year. So I guess I had a good time.

So I roll home slightly tiddly and very happy slightly late to your father's birthday party, everyone there but Numa & Mildred who were also 15 min. late and Wesley is taking care of everything that I had left fully organized for him and I am not so very much appreciated by a certain member, but the party was whoodedoo fun, at least for me, and I had spent all morning making a perfectly magnificent new dessert from the N.Y. Times called "Royal Velvet", and it had kinda oozed and exploded all over the kitchen that morning, but gads, was it good, and I had decided to have it at a Wine Tasting party, too, so I had gotten a bottle each of a St. Julien, a Medoc and a St. Emilion and I used the new Baccarat and I had the lovely green grape centerpiece and everyone raved about the food, so I ate roast & drank wine and talkedtalkedtalkedtalkedtalked. So when everyone left, I got it.

CELESTE MADE NATIONAL HONOR SOCIETY!!!!!!!!!!!

The next night Bill & Dorothy R. had a cocktail party for the Hilsbergs and I distinguished myself, as usual. So after 2 highballs I decide to go see someone across the room so all of a sudden I find myself wading in the fish pond; after the initial shock I relaxed and enjoyed it & lifted up my dress and start roaring with glee and splashed happily thru to the other side, to be rescued by Ben Yancey & Morris Newman. Everyone seemed upset and wanted me to wipe my feet, take off shoes etc. etc., but I said I had Pa. Dutch Peasant feet and I never caught cold, and Ben Yancey said you fall in the pond & I have all of a sudden to have another drink, and Bill came up and said I had joined an honorable society and would receive from him a certificate and I said, Bill, remember when you were planning this dream house 10 yrs. ago I told you NOT TO DO THE POND INSIDE. And then your father came up, and said, Helene, you had better move, so I look down and there I am standing in a suspicious looking puddle so everyone laughs and I leap across the room and Morris said isn't it just like a husband to see something like that, he was the only one, and Chuck Keller said, no Helene I saw it too but I see you do that all the time on the side of my pool, and this is no different. Your father left the party and for the first time conceded SYMPHONY CAN BE FUN!

Celeste & Maury went to Covington and stayed with Randolph and Alice Lyons. Ann went off to Ice Breakers in her lovely new dress that I got her, small madonna blue checked sheer stuff, old-fashioned looking with long sleeves and round neck trimmed with self-ruffles and a wide electric blue velvet sash looking good enough to eat. Crin asked Steffie over today and she arrived with that Ann Field and they went upstairs and did untold damage to the room with mess, and the next thing S. & A. are running off with Crin screaming behind them to go to Steffi's and the next thing 1/2 hour later Crin home crying they had gone to A's house and she was being bitchy. Gads.

We drive across the river today to keep your father company while he was cleaning the gutters, and as I turned into the road, there were two little boys in the middle of it, and a spilled bike, and I leapt out the car and the littlest little boy, about 6, had got his foot caught between the wheels and when I helped get it lose, poor thing screaming he had gashed it to the bone, so I picked him up and put him in my car, and asked where he lived told the other boy to take the bike, so took him home. Later on, Ann, looking out the dormer of our house, said she saw an ambulance go to his house.

  So ends another week.

           Love,
             Ma

Letter 50

pm 2 Nov 59

Dear Gals:

Sorry about missing a week. There had been a kinda upsetting little incident with the Maestro at the opening concert, and these <u>little</u> things seem to affect me big. Well, Lise & I went together, so when it was over, she turned to me and said "What's going on between you and the Maestro?" He had done nothing but look up here at you all night. So I said, silly girl. So, Alvin takes me to the Opening Night party, which, incidentally, was a humdinger, being given in the enclosed patio of that new motel in the Quarter, and it is toujours gai, greeting all my old friends back, and Hilsberg and Madam arrive late, so I go up with an "Oh, lovely, lovely" and he looks at me with those slanting Mongolian eyes and spits out, "I smiled at you three times tonight. Vy did you not smile back?" So, I say "Oh, why of course I smiled back". And get a look from the eyes, so I say, "Oh didn't I smile back. Too busy clapping, I suppose, to smile back. How do you do, Mrs. Hilsberg" And then there is the business that there is no special table for him, no table at all, so I rush around like something crazy and finally find someone to put up another table, and he in the meantime is sitting down at the manager's table, with Mrs. Daley, and Mrs. Hilsberg says to me "TZIT DOWN", so I tzit down, and long apologies and oh, yes of course the table is necessary for tzitting down of the Maestro right away on account of the heart attack last year, so I spread it on very thick, and suddenly she says "And vere are your seats in the Auditorium, Mrs. Hero" as if she had not been glaring at me all last year, so I tell her, and "And vy do you tzit there, Mrs. Hero", so I tell her, and the Maestro comes and tzits down and I just glare at him over his head without saying a word, and as soon as someone else comes up I get up and run, run, run. I am now known in Symphony Circles as "Fish Pond Hero", and everyone who sees me wants to know if I have been swimming lately with all my clothes on.

I took Ann to the concert last week to hear Casadesus, and I had been to the rehearsal with Marilyn in the morning, and we had driven him and Mrs. Bowie to Galatoire's for lunch, so when Ann begged to go back stage to meet him, Mrs. Bowie, who was guarding his door, let us in first, and I told him that Ann had counted the number of pages that were turned while he played the D'Indy, and he said, wait, I will see, so he got his music out of his case, and checked, and said You are right, would you like me to sign your program for you, so she was thrilled.

I picked out some very attractive wall paper for the house across the river. It will be prettier than it is now. For the dining room I chose a chinoiserie looking one, lots of brown stemmed vine that will look well with the wood walls of the living-room, with green leaves, and orangey flowers and a pretty colored bird every now and then, the room that had the television will be in a soft grey-green to match the leaves of the paper, and on the other side of the house, I took to the blues, and chose a small chintzy flowered pattern on blue ground for the front bedroom, a plain blue, light-medium, for the back br and for the bathroom between the usual bathroom fishes on a blue ground. The paper is all much smaller patterned than the ones now there and will look better in the small rooms. Ma's eye has improved, and it took me only 1/2 hour to get it all picked out.

I had to receive at the first woman's do last Friday. Guitar playing & singing of folk songs that rather bored me, but it was very crowded. Whether the people came to hear it, or to see the new Heinemann house in Audubon place one cannot tell. The house is a tremendously expensive eclectic nothing. I escaped right away when it was over, and did not stay for the tea sandwiches, coffee and sherry. I sat on the steps in the hall, and after looking at the ecstatic faces of the audience, I decided there was really no one there I wanted to hang around and talk to. Gad, what a horrid snob I am.

Crin was very unhappy about the two Newman parties she was invited to, because neither one was going trick or treating, so she called up Ann Field to see if she would come Tr. & Tr. with her, and got invited to Ann Fields party. I shall recommend her to the Symphony Society.

Love,   Ma

Letter 51

pm 16 Nov 59

Dear Gals

This week, nothing at all, at all happened. Went across the river with Raymond yesterday. The paper hangers have finished, and Raymond has been doing the woodwork. The woodwork in the dining room will have to be done over as the background of the paper is creamy and it looked all right with the old, yellowish woodwork, but now that Raymond has done it chalk it looks awful. I had really wanted to make what had been the T.V. room a light brownish pink, but was afraid tenants would scream, so the green next to the d r. isn't quite what it should be. However, for being limited to $1.00 a roll paper, it really isn't bad.

Alfred called while I was having coffee at Dannie's so she asked him to stay to lunch and asked me to too and we had some gorgeous oyster soup, cheese sandwiches & wine, and it was lovely and festive and Alfred was entertaining and stimulating, as he always is. I am afraid I stayed too long after, leaving finally at 4, because, after all, he had not come to see me.

Took Maury & Celeste to the concert Tuesday to hear young Michael Rayburn play the violin. I had gone to the rehearsal that morning, and was investigating the possibilities of doing something about the stars' dressing-room, and he was in it, when I went in with Jack Daley, and there was a mirror, and I asked Rayburn if he had brought it in on his back, or what. He is quite young, not at all affected, and was fun to talk too. Daley said it was hopeless to try to do anything, because, as we were not the only ones to use the auditorium, everything that we put in got stolen by someone else. Committee disbanded! Celeste bowled everyone over with her knockout beauty.

The Symphony had a hearing at a Council meeting, to try and get the city to raise its $5,000 allotment back to the original $15,000. All were asked to turn out, but there

Celeste and Ann

were not more than 5 other women beside myself. Bill did not make the plea as he was in Houston, so it was turned over to the General, which was disappointing. Do not know how it came out yet. After it was over, took myself to Pillow Talk, which is a must for sheer fun and slick comedy.

Please make out your Xmas lists right away. The invitations did not come out the way I wanted them, after 2 proofs today just went ahead and printed them, wrong. I have never in my life had so much trouble. They do the Symphony work, and I have heard Marilyn scream about the mistakes and I cannot for the life of me see why she doesn't go somewhere else.

Love,
Ma

[in same envelope]

Dear Gals:

The past week was very quiet. We went down to Geo.'s birthday party, and it was the usual glamorous Madeline party, with candlelight and lots of sparkling burgundy. She has re-arranged her living room in an odd manner, and not a good one, to my way of thinking. It is now rather like a long, narrow hotel lobby, with everything marching down in twos with a table in between, and one sofa facing it all at the very end. It must be her sex-drive coming out; everything a deux. So, since that was the way she wanted it, I sat myself by myself at one of the petite arrangements and ignored the rest of the women at the far end by the facing sofa, and by golly, it works! Pretty soon, I had Nolly and George sitting by me, Geo. pulling up a chair to the a deux to make it a trois. Geo. had said something to me several weeks ago that I always gave him a birthday present that he liked, one especially and individually for him, so that was quite a challenge he had thrown at me, and it was with fear and trembling that I chose at the Garden Shop a good-looking wood & brass modern barometer-thermometer, small, thinking of his small little office room at home to hang it in. When I told your father what I had gotten and asked him if he thought Geo. would be interested, he, of course, said of course not. The last thing Geo. was interested in was a barometer-thermometer. He had never, never seen one in his house in his life. Well, when Geo. opened it, he turned to me and said he had been wanting one for years, and had been looking for one of those antique ones and had never been able to find one. So I said that this would never take place of those, it was only a small modern one, but it would be accurate so he said he had really given up on the antique ones because he could never find one with a mechanism that worked. And Madeline came rushing up and said that truly, truly, I could not have picked anything that he wanted more. Whew! Still have that ax of a challenge for next year!

Mimi, I think it is so exciting that Honey will come visit us. Do not let her go to Florida on the 24th. Can't she stay for the Xmas party? It is such a hum-dinger of an old N.O. kind of fun party, that maybe she might forego Xmas with the family for once, if they will let her and if she wants to. Maury wants to stay over for it. Apparently Xmas is grim at her house; her mother won't buy a record of Carols or anything, but they do have a fire in the living-room fire place for the only time in the year, and that so that they can immediately burn all the Xmas trash! She moved out yesterday, but came back for dinner, and she and Celeste are out to dinner tonight. I think she likes us, I shall miss her very, very much.

Your father & I both think that there is no situation that could possibly come up that between you, Susan and Mary Sue could not be solved with alacrity, so it looks ok for the European driving. Gee, I have sure matured a lot in the past year, what?

You will not be ashamed of your upstairs when you come back. Raymond is doing a bang-up job. Crin's & Ann's room looks almost decent, and we have painted all the doors white, and everything looks, anyway, fresh and neat, if not fancy, and it is an inspiration for Pearl to pick up. Who cared before?

Time to fix supper for your father and Crin; might stop that horrible knock-down, drag out screaming, yelling fight going on between Ann & Crin upstairs. Got Crin's report. Teacher said she was "unique" and then added, in a class of "eager beavers" she is shy! So my magic in bringing up individuals has not been destroyed even tho you and your father make it a constant fight for me to stand up to what I think is the proper way to bring up children. I haven't failed yet! And I only wish all of you had as much faith in me as I had in you!

On the melancholy note, I go fix Crin a sandwich who has just come up with a happy Hi and then a whine, Mother! I'm starving. And Ann is practicing on the new rented piano. Everyone fights over playing it, Celeste, Crin, Maury when she was here, and me. It's great!

Love,
Ma

[in same envelope]

Nov 59
Dear Gals:

Another quiet week. Last night, however, we had dinner with Herbert and Noel Williams and the Russ Monroes and it was loads of fun. I did try to be quiet and not drink too much, and started off with two vermouths only before dinner, and they had rose wine, and then I found myself demanding that Herbert open another bottle. Luckily it was the American and not French, but still -- oh, well, I just ran across an excellent definition of maturity in Bruno Zevi's "Architecture as Space" which defines it as the age at which time every human being and every human message should set itself vaster aims than self-defense. He gives 25 yrs. as the proper age at which this should be done; however, at 46 and one half, I have just decided that that is what I shall henceforth try to do. Anyhow, Herbert is a scream, such imagination, such humor, and sitting next to him at the table we were shrieking and screaming and yowling, and we woke the babies up twice, had all three of them awake and screaming twice, upstairs. Before dinner Lillian Monroe had been telling about how, being a doctor's wife, she had had three weird and new methods of birth, two of them so awful that after they tried them out on her they never, never did them again. The first baby, they broke the bag and then made her trot up and down, up and down, up and down all night long, walk, walk, walk, they said, and the baby will come. Well, it didn't. Well, after dinner, Herbert said POSITIVELY, he had had his very LAST living-room baby, and henceforth he was carrying around a basket with a very clean sheet in it, and a pair of scissors, and whenever any woman started up about HER terrible birth-pains, he was just going to cut the umbilical cord of that conversation then and there.

I managed to find two bed-spreads for Crin and Ann, and of course they had only one single dust-ruffle. I have found the stores depleted of merchandise; even supercal sheets, only 2. I got some dacron and cotton material in the dress dept. on sale for 88 cents a yd. and am going to have some simple, straight curtains made to hang on the inside of the window frames so they will act as shades too. I am tired of living in a perfect gold-fish bowl of a house. I also got some red and white checked gingham to cover the rocker in Crin & Ann's room. When all of this will be done, I have no idea. Will contact Mrs. Tolarge tomorrow.

Mimi, Frank Eshleman called tonight that the Elves will be calling on you on Sun. Dec 20th. I accepted. You will be home then, won't you? Town & Country never delivered your dress. Should I see about it. Hel, the knit shop called me last week that they were sending your sweater, so you must have it by now.

Ann had a slumber party of 8 on Fri. night. I had thought that she was having it on Sat. and had ordered her cake for that day, so Fri. afternoon, we dashed up to Shields and bought another. And at 12 I heard "Happy Birthday" in the kitchen, and her friends had surprised her with a cake and presents!

All quiet on the children-front upstairs. Ann liked all the cards she got. Crin was tickled pink with the one she got for Ann that said I want to kiss you on your Happy Birthday, and on the next page, where is it? That is a one we shall all have to watch. You should see her jitterbug! I have to sneak outside and watch her thru a window; she won't let me look at her.

Ma.

Letter 52

pm 12 Jan 60

Dear Gals:

Dolly and Frank came over to see Hel yesterday and we had a lot of fun on the side porch. He is going to Dutch New Guinea to mine diamonds. I truly like the guy a lot; one of these people with tremendous imagination and great humor and his stories are marvelous. Quite adult for his age, too. Walter's summation of him seems so wild; and all those wild stories that really made me sick, I am completely dismissing. Dolly's charm charms me more every time I see her.

The 1812 Ball was wild and wonderful Sat. night. First time in 4 years we have been, and a new bunch has joined, and we sat up and matched degeneracies. I have never laughed so hard. Gar Moore, who runs the race track, and his wife, who is one of the owners of the Knit Shop were at our table and they are both screamingly funny. I was doubled over with some of Gar's understated and dry jokes. I went over to some youngster I never saw before and asked him if he didn't know at least one of my three beautiful daughters and he said name them and when I got to Celeste he said oh, I know HER, so I said what's the matter aren't you the elite, you can't be or else you would be on my Xmas list and I had never seen him before and where did he live, on Mag. street, no, he said 2818 St. Charles, so I said very, very acceptable, will send you an invitation next year, as I was procuring for my daughters.

Tomorrow night Fenella is having a do at the Pontchartrain. Danny has asked Alvin & me to be godparents. The baby is simply lovely, little and dainty. We are thrilled. For some reason Clarisse Grima asked us to a cocktail party Sun. (She's Ike's vintage-bonne Creole, who designed and built her own house in Suburbia.) Ah well, all groups, all groups!!!!!!!

Hel, all this is no news to you, as you just left yesterday. The Wedding was really pretty, very simple and fast. The reception was fun and Muffy Slatten's mother invited herself to our Xmas party next year. Said she can't stand HEARING about it any longer. Martha Miles issued one of her command invitations Sat. so went over, and we have decided to be friends, she said, hell, she had every intention of using my house instead of the Orleans Club for both daughters' debuts and weddings, so she had no intention of letting me stay an enemy. Said our party is really the talk of the town this year. Am trying to get enthusiastic about having Hilsberg and the violinist over next week, but have gone just dead on the Symphony and wish it were over.

Love, Ma.

> Miss Celeste Hero, daughter of Mr. and Mrs. Alvin Hero, home for the holidays from Smith college in North Hampton, Mass., and Miss Susan Breit, daughter of Mr. and Mrs. Hjalmar Breit Jr., who attends Newcomb college, were the honorees Christmas evening at the yearly old-fashioned Christmas party at which Mr. and Mrs. Hero are hosts at their Third st. Garden District home. The reception rooms of the handsome old residence were decked with holly, pine and other seasonal greenery and a large brightly trimmed yule tree stood in one corner. The guests included close friends of the hosts, the honorees and other members of the Hero family.

Letter 53

pm 25 Jan 60

Dear Gals

A letter at last! I have gone and gotten myself very much involved again in the Women's Committee, in more of an emotional way. I figured out a snappy move that reduced the commitment of $12,500 to $9,500 and Bill is in a rage with me. He came here Tuesday night for the party for Morini and took a nasty and devious dig at me, which I instantly caught, and it started me on one of those awful harangues of self-justification for about 15 or 20 minutes, much to his embarrassment. He point-blank told me he doubted my loyalty, so I asked him if he wanted me to resign; he said no. Well, what I did, to me, in no way affects anything if we can make $12,500 with the two Benefits planned; but if we don't make it, it is merely a little safe-facing or face-saving, but he doesn't see it that way. And I got up at the Board meeting Wed. and suggested a note of thanks to Eileen Wilson for past work done; this when the race-track fell through again. It was greeted with a wall of silence, and made everyone hate me, which I knew it would, but the Chairman said she would write one. So I called Bill and told him that woman could produce if handled right, but it would now have to come from the men, and he blew his top at me and called her a rotten apple and said he was through with her. However, Marilyn who has been drilling into Eileen to do this thing, told me he had called her that night after my call and is taking her to the Symphony Tues. Marilyn is convinced Eileen is going to come thru. Gads, I have been in bed! So I see Bill at M.L.'s last night and he is all over me like a wet wash rag: Oh, I yelled at my old friend, Helene, and I said: Well, I yelled right back, Bill, and I promise you I am keeping off the telephone and will never bother you again. But Marilyn & I were really trying very hard to get $10,000 for him and he said $12,500, and I said, oh, no, what we are trying to do is get some gravy for you over and above the $12,500.

My party was a success, I think; gave them Gumbo, salad, cheeses and made that pretty pineapple dessert with Kirsch, and I heard Mr. Hilsberg tell Madam that the best food in New Orleans was to be had in this house. Marilyn came thru with an extra man for me, and he turned out to be a good friend of Henry Hope's -- Alfred Moire, who is teaching art at Newcomb and he was supposed to have gone to Margaret's dinner and he had dinner with Henry the night after. He is most attractive, but he spent the entire night trying to reduce me and slapping me down with insults. The party just suddenly was over, before coffee and liqueurs, because Madam was tired, and mostly upset because the house had been so small and the applause thin. Alfred and Marilyn came back after taking her home, and Steve Hewett also stayed, and we sat in front of the fireplace sipping brandy until 2, so all in all it turned out to be most pleasant. Alfred said something very amusing ----- He came into the living room and said It's not that this is such a charming house or the decorations pretty, it's because it's the only house I have been in that ever had a free standing john!

      Love,
       Ma

Little Room Where Late Night Parties Often Ended Up

Letter 54

pm 15 Mar 60

Dear Gals:

Really, life is dull. I spend my time soaking my bottom all day long, and making trips to Butzie's office thrice weekly. We have not been to a party in so long that my brain feels washed clean, dull and empty. I don't think I could carry on a conversation of more than one syllable words; possibly baby-talk. I have been being a good mother, seeing that Crin eats, bathes and sleeps and she seems to be coming out of that awful spell she had. I can yell at her again instead of being polite to her.

I finally gave in to Ann and am having a juke box party of 80 7 graders Sat. night. May the saint in heaven who protects protect. The phone calls began tonight -- 20 down, 60 more to come.

Crin is thrilled because she has been put into "Script Group", which means she can now do all her writing in script. It has meant a lot to her, and she came home and told me something wonderful had happened to her. Ann made an A on the weather report that she struggled so terribly hard on; it was completed in spite of spilled ink, many new starts, me frantically hunting a city suddenly run dry of poster paper at 6 on Sat. tears, smears and smudges. It goes to Tulane to the Science Contest, and if it passes that, to the State contest.

Celeste went to a Pi K.A. dance Sat. and had a very good time. Went across the river yesterday; the yard looks a deal better. We have planted, guess -- BAMBOO -- to cut the size of the yard down. Saw Danny -- she gave a dress for whomever it fitted. It fitted Celeste, but unfortunately it is printed in red and purple flowers. Celeste thinks Maury would like it.

Can't wait for you-all to come home.

                          Love,
                              Ma

Letter 55

pm 27 Apr 60

Dear Hel

I do miss your most beautiful, cheerful smiling face & presence so much. What a wonderful gal you are.

Suddenly I am really on the road to recovery. In the middle of the night, night before last, I broke into a terrific sweat, & suddenly I felt almost well. I have had no fever since, but I am a pretty tottering wreck.

Pearl left, just like that, a week before she was supposed to, and just as your father was going to ask her on Mon. to delay her leaving another week. Zoom -- gone -- just didn't show up Mon. Mary, of course, knew all about it and has fortunately corralled a church-singing cohort to come work for us. Your pa says she has a mouth full of gold buck teeth. I shall be completely & hopelessly helpless in their hands. However, thanks be to Jesus for her at this time.

Dolly called to see how I was & said she & Iris wanted to come see me & I think I hurt her feelings by saying I wanted no visitors. She said she was leaving Friday for summer & wanted to see me before she left. What a lovely child she is! She took Crin out all Sunday -- Celeste said she & Linny & Iris & Dolly & Jim scrambled eggs, had wine at the house afterwards. I am glad Celeste is now an acccptcd mcmbcr of the group.

Thanks again for everything you did. My attitude toward life is a great deal cheerier now that I no longer feel sick -- pain & penicillin can distort as badly as, I imagine, does opium.

Love,
Ma.

PS I have even forgiven Butzie! He is much   relieved that

I smile at him once more. I think his attitude is due to the fact that it kills him to think he is causing pain to anyone he loves, and he does love us!

Letter 56

pm 9 May 60

Dear Gals:

I am sitting in bed, listening to my new FM radio; it's delightful! Now your father and I don't have to fight. Not that we did, I just never heard the music I liked. It's a his-her deal, one on each side of the bed, and as all I listen to is music, it furnishes the background to his news-broadcasts. Perfect. My broadcasting date is Fri. May 27th, and if ever I get out of this bed of recuperation, I am going to go to the studio and look it over and find out what my broadcasting will be, and Marilyn is going to help me with the pronunciations, if needed. I know I'll be better than the three I have heard so far -- and that is not conceit -- they are lousy! I think it will be a lot of fun, and hope they call on me again.

I got home Monday, weak, weak, And of course, the leader of the church quartet, Alberta by name, whom Mary had gotten to come to work, did not show up. Called that she had quit, later in the day. So we have no one, and we are doing beautifully, and the house has never been so clean, and Crin is learning to do things, and I get out of bed and putter for an hour, in bed for three, out for another, and presto! mess all gone. I am enjoying my servantless status, really. Celeste and Ann pinch-hit as cooks, and it really has cut down on the fighting. Crin still yells when told to do something, but when I get back on my feet, I intend to wear her down. She is really lately a changed person. Guess what she said! She asked me if I thought I would have to go back to the hospital, and I said I had firmly made up my mind not to, and anyway I had stayed this time 11 days instead of 3, and she said, yes, because I let you, and giggled, so I giggled and we both just giggled and giggled. I just love having your father bring my breakfast in bed, with a posy he picked. And I find myself just as querulous as James Rogers was if it isn't just to my liking.

And I like really seeing no one. No upsetting lunches with female friends who give subtle nasty digs that one mulls over afterwards, no too much talking, no too much complaining and whining. Well, how long I will last so pure remains to be seen, but I am enjoying it!!!!!!!

Poor Weeze is in a bad way. Aesophagitus, or some such outlandish thing, which means an abscess of the Aesophagus, and its almost like an ulcer, and she can't drink smoke or eat and is about out of her mind. If a month of diet does not cure it, it will be an operation for her, too. I think I got the better part of this illness bargain. Hel, congratulations on the wonderful marks. Gads, what brains!

Love, Ma, who knows the therapeutic
value of house work

Letter 57

pm 30 May 60

Dear Gals:

Well, the last letter of the year! This time next week we shall all be together, and I am getting excited.

No news. I have been very quiet, no excitement and seeing scarcely anyone. Going out to the Yacht Club by myself and book and swimming. Took K. Danna once last week. Offered her some sun oil, oh no, with horror, I simply bathe every day with E. Arden's Body Oil. I don't need sun oil, making me feel slimy. A couple of nights ago Jim invited me to come down to Kolb's and it was a lot of fun sitting around a couple of hours with him and Celeste and Jim Carlton and Dev. Danna and drinking white wine and laughing and laughing.

I did my disk-jockey job and got thru it with the help of your father, who helped me put on the records, write the log and see that I manipulated the controls ok. I just plain busted out in hives. It was opera night and I had lots to read; the synopsis of the story Mignon, besides the commercials. They just turn the entire thing over to you, no one else is there, and I had had an hour's instruction Wed. afternoon. If they ask me back it will not be so bad.

My Mobile cousin on 2nd street, Lila Binnings, called up out of the blue and invited us over to a very pleasant kind of neighborhood get-together, simple, not large, no trouble, and just nice to see people without getting wildly drunk and in fights and going home after two drinks.

    Gee, do you think I am getting MATURE?

                           Love,
                              Ma

Leone Rothschild took the Chairmanship of the Women's Comm. strictly out of a sense of duty. She looked pea green sick about it at the Ex. Board meeting and tried to sell me the job again twice. The first thing she did was have a motion passed that the W.C. refused to give any more benefits!!!!! We shall tell the men we no longer will allow them to put us arbitrarily down for $12,500 a year. Gads, what is Bill going to say about her. The final meeting is here Wed. She called yesterday and offered me a choice of jobs. Have to take something as she helped me so, but told her to throw something small at me, I hated it all and couldn't choose.

No Longer Chair, Still Giving Parties

Letter 58

[no envelope -- early 1962]

Dear Gals:

Well, I don't know where I left off in the news. Did I tell you about the wonderful upholstered chair I found for Mimi and John on Magazine St. for $5.00? It's on a small scale, but extremely comfortable, has lovely lines, straight spaded legs, very Sheridan in look. They started Sun. doing it over themselves; taking off the old upholstery, and the old varnish and sandpapering it. I told them to call Walter Stauf[fer] about how to refinish it, because I had gotten a wonderful formula from him when I did over the top of my old dining-room table, and I still had the stuff left over that he gave me but I had lost the instructions. So Mimi called him, and she and John started in on the first step last night. So far, she has not found any material to cover it.

John Le Bourgeois, Mimi's Fiancé

I told you that when Mimi told me John was going to give her an engagement ring I said I never had heard anything more ridiculous in my life, and one night when we were all sitting in the kitchen she told him what I had said, and his mouth flew open in complete amazement, so I said, there I go, being an interfering mother-in-law already, just forget what I said. Well, two or three nights later, Mimi came to me and said John had been thinking it over, and thought it was really a good idea and not to spend the $300 or so he had for a ring, but to buy a painting instead. So they have been shopping around, but a picture is hard to find. So I thought of Mr. Flettrich, whose paintings I myself have never seen, but he is a good friend of the Alferezes and I have heard from a number of people that he is good, so I called him up yesterday, introduced myself, said I had met him -- blank went the name Alferez, so he said quickly, I met you at your house. I said, you did, when, and he said, don't you remember that time that Isaac Stern gave that lecture at your house, and the plane was late? Well, I was the one who met him at the airport and brought him to your house. So I told him the reason I was calling him, and I just wanted to find out from him where would be the best place to go to see his paintings, and said here in my studio, and to come Wed. night at 8:30, and for me to come too, and he would have a one man showing for three people. So it all sounds fun, but John seemed worried about suppose they didn't like anything, and I said not to worry about that, that I had told him you two were looking around, and just put it on the basis that they are only walking into a shop, that an artist is naturally anxious to sell, and that we are doing him a favor, even if they don't buy.

The LeBourgeois had us over the other night, with Mamsie and Louis. John and Charless, his brother, also paint, but in an entirely different manner. Charless' things are full of a sense of humor and a sense of the ridiculous, with any odd, strange little figures, some of them full of horror. I had heard a great deal about Charless, how strange and silent he was, and his mother said she considered three whole words from him a complete sentence, usually it's yes, no, unhun. Well, Charless blew in, got introduced, disappeared, came slamming through again, and Mimi turned to John and said where on earth is Charless going, and John said, I don't know, and I said I just bet he spends his time slamming in and out of here like that all the time without a word to anyone and also that you just don't dare ask him a question. Well, when we were leaving, I saw Charless sitting in a chair in his room, so I went in and said, in the bathing trunks just as I have heard, and do you mean to tell me I can believe all those mean and nasty things I have heard about you? So he stood up and said, yes, you can believe them, I am really a very mean and nasty person, so I said, so am I, and he said, in that case we shall be friends, and I said, that there was no doubt about it, that anyone who had the sense of humor and the sense of the ridiculous that he had and that so obviously showed on all these things hanging on the walls I would just be bound to like.

Mr. LeBourgeois is very upset because the men are not going to wear tails in the wedding, because it is the proper thing to do at a 7 o'clock wedding. So I just told him hard, fast, and mean that this was going to be a very simple small house wedding, and I'd be Goddammed if I would allow any rule in an etiquette book to force me into making it an elaborate affair. So he said, well, let's make it at 6:30, we'll be half right, and I said, No Sir, the invitations are already ordered and I'd be dammed if I was going to change them, so I had him sitting around biting his fingernails for the rest of the night.

I was talking to Mamsie about Mrs. Claiborne's baby basket, and how after Caroline got too large for it, I had tried to return it to her, but she said just to keep it, there was no one else in the family to have children right now, and if ever she needed it again she would know where it was. So I told Mamsie, that I would just turn over the baby basket to John and Mimi, now that we had become some kind of in-laws, so John quoted something from Chaucer to the effect about how children made you lose your sense of humor, and took all the joy out of life, so I said, oh dear, do you mean you two aren't going to make me a grandmother, what a shame. And all of a sudden Mamsie clutched my arm and hissed in my ear, this is awful, this perfectly awful, talking about these two having children when they aren't even married yet! I was so stunned, I just said, oh, yes isn't it, we must stop it immediately. Well, the next morning Mimi came chuckling into my room and said John had it all figured out about that 7 months baby Mamsie had, and I groaned, innocent little me, such a thing never occurred to me and I had whanged into her sensitive spot. [John was wrong, it was a 9 month baby.] She also was talking about going for a ride in my grandmother's limousine, and I said, that wasn't my grandmother's limousine, that was a funeral parlor car, and Chere rented it with always the same chauffeur by name of August whenever she went out. Dead silence from Mamsie. So I said, Now Mamsie, don't tell me that that is going to make my grandmother lose status in your eyes. But brother, it did. I had shocked her all the way down to her silly little social toes.

   To the dentist.
          Love,
             Ma and Hel

Letter 59

[post card from Paris, France avec "Vue générale de la Place de la Concorde", n.d.]

Your father is walking me very rapidly past the beautiful shops on the Rue de la Paix! I may get in one, but I haven't much hope!

                Love,
                    Mother

EPILOGUE

As these letters reveal, Hélène felt life intensely. When her tenure as chair ended, she became depressed. Diagnosis of mental illness was still confused in the 1960's and treatments inadequate, but it's now clear that she was bipolar. On April 21, 1965, refusing to be a burden to her family, she committed suicide.

WOMAN, 52, DIES IN 6-FLOOR FALL

Body Found on Roof of Touro Extension

Mrs. Alvin A. Hero, of 1213 Third, jumped or fell to her death from the seventh floor of Touro Infirmary about 8 a. m. Wednesday, police said. She was 52.

Her body was found on the roof of a one-story extension facing Delachaise st.

Mrs. Hero had been admitted to the hospital's psychiatric ward last week after taking an overdose of barbiturates, police said.

Mrs. Hero was last seen alive Wednesday while she was drinking coffee in the infirmary's sixth floor lounge between 7:30 and 7:45 a. m.

A nurse began looking for Mrs. Hero; then assistant housekeeper Peter Guidry discovered a body lying on the first floor roof.

Police said there is a wooden scissors gate at the top of the stairs leading to the roof, which would be easily opened or climbed over.

The stairs are part of a fire well leading from the psychiatric unit. A hospital official said fire regulations forbid the locking of the stairway.

Mrs. Hero was pronounced dead on the scene.

INDEX OF NAMES

Alfred and Barbara Hero: Alfred was Alvin's nephew, a West Point graduate and director of the World Peace Foundation in Boston. Barbara was an artist. They invited Walter to live with them in Cambridge when Harvard had no dorm room for him.

Alvin Hero: Hélène's husband. Partner with George Hero, Jr in Comfortair Company, a mechanical and electrical contracting company they founded after WW II. Also Alvin was a partner in Hero Lands with his siblings Alfred, Numa, Fenella, George and Claire. Their father, George Alfred Hero, Sr. bought land in Plaquemines Parish around 1912 to drain the West Bank for development.

Bill Ricciuti: New Orleans architect, Chairman of Philharmonic Symphony Board, married to Hélène's school friend, Dorothy.

Butzie Danna, MD: Hélène's doctor, was married to her childhood friend Katherine Deveraux. They were close friends.

Celeste Lyons Offutt: Hélène's first cousin. A civil rights activist, she helped integrate New Orleans public schools.

Dannie and George Hero III: Alvin's nephew and his wife. Dannie was a writer and TV producer in the early days of WDSU. George worked under Werner von Braun with the US Missile Program before NASA was established. Later was a partner at Comfortair Company, then became a forensic engineer in the field of mechanical and electrical failures.

DePaul's: Mental hospital.

Devlin, Miss: Principal of the Lower School at Newman.

Dreyfus, Miss Ruth: Psychologist at Newman School.

Dolly Jordan: neighbor and friend of Hero girls.

Emmy Walker: friend of young Hélène and her sisters.

Ike and Hélène Stauffer: Hélène's father and mother; he was President of Stauffer Eshleman Wholesale Hardware Co. In 1922 they bought the Hurst Plantation on Tchoupitoulas Street, New Orleans, and moved it to 3 Garden Lane, Metairie.

Jack McIlhenny: Hélène's second cousin, of the Tabasco family. His mother was Anita Stauffer McIlhenny.

Lise Wherman Todd: Hélène's best friend from school days.

Lou Stauffer: Hélène's unmarried aunt, Ike's sister.

Madeline and George Hero: George was Alvin's brother, Madeline his wife. A partner in Comfortair and in Hero Lands.
Mamsie and Louis LeBourgeois: Louis was John's uncle. His wife Mamsie knew the Stauffers because her mother,

Mrs. Claiborne, was a friend of Hélène's aunt Lou Stauffer. It was through them that the custom of passing a baby basket between the families got started.

Marie Celeste Lyons or MC: Hélène's aunt and Celeste Offutt's mother. She was bipolar.

Marie Louise (Weeze, M.L.) and Warren Posey: Marie Louise was Hélène's younger sister and Warren was her husband, an advertising executive.

Marilyn Barnett: Symphony Women's Committee friend, tennis champion, conducted classical music program on WNPS.

Martha and Porcher Miles: friends of Hélène and Alvin. Alvin married Martha after both Porcher and Hélène died. In Letter 52 Martha said she wanted her daughters to be married at Hélène's house, and after Alvin married her they both were.

Mary: longtime laundress.

Maury Offutt: Daughter of Celeste Offutt and Celeste Hero's friend.

McGhee School: Hélène's private girls' school, at the time known more for its elite students than for academic rigor. She didn't finish Newcomb College, having to leave when her father lost money during the depression.

Melvin: longtime gardener.

Molly and Barney McCloskey, Walter McCloskey: Molly was Hélène's second cousin. Barney, her husband, was Commissioner of Public Safety of New Orleans and Walter is their son. Walter couldn't get a dorm room as a freshman at Harvard so he lived with Alfred and Barbara Hero that year.

Numa, Jr. and Mildred Hero: Alvin's nephew and his wife. Numa worked at Hero Lands in Plaquemines Parish.

Pearl: longtime housekeeper and cook.

Quins, Harlequins, Elves of Oberon, Mystic and Comus are all carnival balls. The men members send Call Outs to women they plan to dance with.

Raymond Van Court: longtime handy man and painter.

Schultz, Mrs. Edwina: Principal of Upper School at Newman.

Vicky and Virginia Kelly: Vicky was young Hélène's close school friend and Virginia was her mother.

Made in the
USA
Monee, IL